TARZAN AND TRADITION

Erling B. Holtsmark

TARZAN AND TRADITION

Classical Myth in Popular Literature

CONTRIBUTIONS TO THE STUDY OF POPULAR CULTURE,
NUMBER 1

Greenwood Press
WESTPORT, CONNECTICUT • LONDON, ENGLAND

Library of Congress Cataloging in Publication Data

Holtsmark, Erling B   1936–
   Tarzan and tradition.

   (Contributions to the study of popular culture ;
no. 1 ISSN 0198-9871)
      Bibliography: p.
      Includes index.
      1.   Burroughs, Edgar Rice, 1875–1950—Criticism and
interpretation.   2.   Tarzan.   3.   Fantastic fiction,
American—History and criticism.   I.   Title.   II.   Series.
   PS3503.U687Z7   813'.52   80-1023
   ISBN 0-313-22530-3 (lib. bdg.)

Library of Congress Catalog Card Number: 80-1023
ISBN: 0-313-22530-3
ISSN: 0198-9871

First published in 1981

Greenwood Press
A division of Congressional Information Service, Inc.
88 Post Road West, Westport, Connecticut 06881

Printed in the United States of America

10 9 8 7 6 5 4 3 2 1

ACKNOWLEDGMENTS

Deep appreciation is expressed to the following publishers and agents for permission to reprint:

To Brigham Young University Press, extracts from Irwin Porges, *Edgar Rice Burroughs: The Man Who Created Tarzan* (Provo, Utah: Brigham Young University Press, 1975).

To Marion T. Burroughs, vice-president of Edgar Rice Burroughs, Inc., for gracious permission to cite necessary material from the following books:
   Tarzan of the Apes, copyright 1912 by The Frank A. Munsey Co., copyright renewed by Edgar Rice Burroughs, Inc.
   The Return of Tarzan, copyright 1913 by Street & Smith, copyright renewed by Edgar Rice Burroughs, Inc.
   The Beasts of Tarzan, copyright 1914 by The Frank A. Munsey Co., copyright renewed by The Frank A. Munsey Co.
   The Son of Tarzan, copyright 1915, 1916 by The Frank A. Munsey Co.
   Tarzan and the Jewels of Opar, copyright 1916 by The Frank A. Munsey Co., copyright renewed by The Frank A. Munsey Co.
   Jungle Tales of Tarzan, copyright 1916, 1917 by Story-Press Corporation, copyright renewed by The McCall Corporation.

To George Chambers, publisher, Arizona Silhouettes, for permission to cite from the Preface of *Life Among the Apaches* by John Cremony (first published in 1868; reprint, Tucson, Arizona: Arizona Silhouettes, 1951).

To Philosophical Library, Inc., for permission to cite from Paul Radin, *The Trickster: A Study in American Indian Mythology* (New York: Bell Publishing Co., Inc., 1956).

To Pitman Publishing Limited, for citations from Lord Raglan, *The Hero: A Study in Tradition, Myth and Drama* (New York: Watts, 1956).

To Princeton University Press for a citation from Eric S. Rabkin, *The Fantastic in Literature* (Princeton, N.J.: Princeton University Press, 1976).

To Leland Sapiro, editor, *Riverside Quarterly*, for use of a citation from *Riverside Quarterly* 4, no. 2 (January 1970).

To many students, past, present, and future;
to their parents;
to the people of Iowa.

EPIGRAPHS

Χάρις δ', ἄπερ ἅπαντα τεύχει τὰ μείλιχα θνατοῖς,
ἐπιφέροισα τιμὰν καὶ ἄπιστον ἐμήσατο πιστόν
ἔμμεναι τὸ πολλάκις,
ἀμέραι δ' ἐπίλοιποι
μάρτυρες σοφώτατοι.

The charms of poetry which makes all pleasant things for mortals, by adding glory contrive that even the unbelievable be believable—often! Days to come are the most skilled witnesses.

Pindar, Olympian I.30–34

Nam ceterae neque temporum sunt neque aetatum omnium neque locorum; at haec studia adulescentiam acuunt, senectutem oblectant, secundas res ornant, adversis perfugium ac solacium praebent, delectant domi, non impediunt foris, pernoctant nobiscum, peregrinantur, rusticantur.

Other forms of relaxation are not connected with all our circumstances, periods in life, and places of activity. But this pursuit that is literature whets our youth and delights our old age; it embellishes our times of prosperity and offers a source of refuge and solace when things go against us; it brings us pleasure in the privacy of our home, yet does not interfere with us in the execution of our public obligations; and it spends the nights with us when we cannot sleep, travels to foreign lands with us, and accompanies us when we sojourn in the country.   Cicero, Pro Archia 16

Every human season creates its storyteller. When the world grows suddenly larger and the old myths shrivel and seem to wither away, he arrives somehow to tell his tale. If he is a great storyteller, his story tells all the things the people feel but can never say, not even to themselves. If he is merely good, he tells only part of the story they long to hear, and years may pass before another storyteller comes along to complete the tale. But great or good, he is always popular—for however disguised his story is, however fantastic it may seem, its true subject is the single one that interests all mankind, Reality.

Edgar Rice Burroughs was a storyteller . . .

Richard Kyle, *Riverside Quarterly* 4.2
(January 1970): 110

CONTENTS

PREFACE

I come to this study as a professional classicist, and I bring to it methods similar to those I apply to classical literature. This procedure lends itself to the study of Burroughs' novels precisely because they are conceived and to a large extent executed in a manner that speaks of a classical background and classical influences.

Steering a course somewhere between popularization and scholarship, I shall address myself not only to classicist but also to professional and nonprofessional students of literature. In no sense am I engaging in a form of intellectual slumming.

For purposes of citation, I have used the following shortened forms in referring to the novels: *Tarzan* (*Tarzan of the Apes*, 1912), *Return* (*The Return of Tarzan*, 1913), *Beasts* (*The Beasts of Tarzan*, 1914), *Son* (*The Son of Tarzan*, 1915), *Jewels* (*Tarzan and the Jewels of Opar*, 1916), and *Tales* (*Jungle Tales of Tarzan*, 1916). In referring to specific passages cited, I use one number (1 = *Tarzan*, 2 = *Return*, 3 = *Beasts*, 4 = *Son*, 5 = *Jewels*, and 6 = *Tales*) followed a period and another number referring to the page of the text in the Ballantine Books paperback edition that was first printed in July 1963; subsequent printings have maintained the identical pagination. All references and citations from Burroughs' Tarzan texts in this book are from the following Ballantine Books, Inc., printings: *Tarzan*, sixth printing (November 1972); *Return*, sixth printing (November 1972); *Beasts*, fourth printing (November 1972); *Son*, sixth printing (April 1975); *Jewels*, sixth printing (April

1975); and *Tales,* sixth printing (April 1975). A reference such as 4.18, for example, means page 18 of *The Son of Tarzan.*

I would like to acknowledge my sincere debt to Edgar Rice Burroughs, Inc. of Tarzana, California, and especially to Mrs. Marion T. Burroughs, vice-president, for graciously granting permission to use the name Tarzan in the title of this book and to cite freely from the novels. Needless to say, neither Edgar Rice Burroughs, Inc. nor any others mentioned in this preface bear any responsibility for what is said in the book.

I wish also to thank the Graduate College of the University of Iowa for making available to me the services of two research assistants: Martha Bowers, who has my warmest thanks for an exemplary job in running down widely scattered bibliographic materials in this library and through interlibrary loan; and Dennis Haltinner, who deserves credit for other editorial help. Keith Rageth, interloan librarian at the University of Iowa, was extremely helpful in the acquisition of necessary materials, and I thank him and his staff. Harlan Sifford, art librarian at the university, aided in ways that perhaps he himself does not realize. To the secretary of the Department of Classics, Jane Davis, I offer my gratitude for so cheerfully consenting to type several earlier and longer drafts from messy copies.

Various people have read versions of this manuscript and have made candid suggestions for improvements. I am indebted to them all for forcing me to rethink certain points of style and substance. Six people should be singled out.

Since the inception of this project, Diana Robin has expressed sustained interest and enthusiasm for it, and that indirect encouragement has served me well on a number of occasions. Carol Klaes read the entire introduction and first chapter in an early draft and gave wise counsel for needed corrections. Professor Charles Altman of the Department of French and Italian and Professor Archibald Coolidge of the Department of English at the University of Iowa have read portions of this manuscript and have given prudent and conscientious advice, for which I thank them. Mrs. Birgit Holtsmark read the full text of an earlier draft and offered useful thoughts on pruning away the excesses. I also would like to thank Betty Pessagno for her thorough editing and sensible criticism of the final manuscript.

Most of all, however, I would like to register my deep gratitude to Professor Dee Lesser Clayman of the Department of Classics at Brooklyn College, City University of New York, who not only gave me material and moral support at a time when it was very much needed but also read most of the original manuscript and shared with me her very cogent thinking on it: *gratias ago iucundissimas.*

Finally, the people to whom this book is dedicated have earned some recognition. Students often have to work to pay my salary, their parents almost always do, and the people who pay the Iowa tax man have no choice. These individuals should be thanked for supporting the fine university system of which I am privileged to be a part. They have made this work possible. I salute the dedicands of this book: they put my family's bread on the table, and they butter it.

I am thankful for this.

TARZAN AND TRADITION

INTRODUCTION

Those critics who have acknowledged Edgar Rice Burroughs have not at all been kind to him. In a review of one Tarzan movie, a writer makes the following typical comment about the novel, "I have never (I say it without pride) read *Tarzan of the Apes*. But I can well believe that it is a nauseating work. . . ."[1] Another critic gives this thumbnail analysis, " . . . the appeal of the Tarzan stories was and is certainly not a literary one, for Burroughs just about totally ignored all the basic rules of style, grammar and syntax. To say that his writing was technically inept would be an understatement. . . ."[2]

The reasons for the hostility to Burroughs' works are many and seem to display recognizable patterns. One of these patterns falls into the category of language and style. Most critical opinion is negative about his English, although some have compared it to that of Henry James and Joseph Conrad.[3] More typical, however, is the condescending observation by a reviewer who speaks of Burroughs' prose as "that loose fustian of the cheap newspapers which is a literary standard for millions."[4] This vein is mined by others who find "no visible trace of style"; who claim that "as to literary style, none is needed. There isn't time"; [5] who praise with the not so faint condemnation that "we must explain the astounding success of a book not through originality of subject matter, but through appealing treatment, even if the appeal in this case is of the lower order."[6]

Perhaps Kingsley Amis is directing his barbs at this matter of style when, somewhat despairingly, he speaks of Burroughs' "dreadfully fluent pen."[7] Another critic manages to excoriate not only the author, but also the reader.

The modern half-educated reader is incapable of understanding a paragraph containing more than a single sentence: the modern writer is apt to get into serious difficulties as soon as he ventures upon a subsidiary clause; thus we have two excellent reasons for keeping our paragraphs as short as possible. Mr. Burroughs does this throughout.[8]

The carping about the improbability of Burroughs' fiction in both the Tarzan stories and the Martian and Venerian accounts is extremely tiresome. Such literal-minded critics are forever tied to the concrete world and will never understand that landscape may also be a matter of interior geography. If the criterion for acceptable literature is verisimilitude to the real world, not only must Homer be discarded, but also much else of the world's greatest literature, including the Bible. Reality, as Plato long ago intimated, is not necessarily that which we see or apprehend with our senses.

If one reads literature, one tacitly renounces certain claims and expectations. There are times when the suspension of disbelief must be willingly and ungrudgingly granted, for otherwise the fiction simply will not work. Homer's *Odyssey*, for example, regales us with an incredible and fantastic series of events that could never be construed as "real," yet the poem deals rigorously with "reality." It comes down, finally, to a question of what one will accept in a literary creation.

Literature that is fantastic by design requires some form of mental or emotional compromise on the reader's part. While the reader recognizes that in the real world of his everyday experience there are many things that do not happen, he can accept them in the fictive world of literature. Eric S. Rabkin puts the matter quite well in his book on the element of the fantastic in literature: "Unless one participates sympathetically in the ground rules of a narrative world, no occurrence in that world can make sense or even nonsense."[9] It can only be an astounding naiveté about fantastic literature that leads a critic to object to the Tarzan narrative on the grounds that the material is anthropologically inaccurate, botanically inexact, or psychiatrically unsuitable.[10]

The matter of Burroughs' prejudices, especially his alleged racism, is also a frequent topic for critics. From the vantage of the late 1970s, Burroughs has a patronizing attitude towards blacks, but to suggest that he was overtly racist is unfair. His attitudes reflect the age in which he lived. Although that does not make them right by contemporary standards, neither is it cause for blanket condemnation. As one scholar has pointed out regarding the views of Burroughs and many of his contemporaries, their thinking on matters of race and religion was not of their own devising but merely reflection of so-called truths that contemporary academicians believed to have been proven objectively.[11] "The collective representations of other cultures are strengthened through the medium of popular fiction but grounded in the scholarship of the period."[11] Burroughs' prejudices, insofar as they exist, are not selective. At times he is (by contemporary standards) outrageously sexist in his presentation of women and has a very low opinion of organized religion, politicians, and lawyers and bureaucratic civilization, to mention a few of his targets. Confronted, as so many others have been, by the apparent paradox of the enormous popularity of a writer seemingly so despicable, one reviewer makes the following comment about the success of the novels: " . . . they sell because they present in the crude forms assimilable by the crude tastes and intelligences of their special public certain commodities which are in themselves by no means contemptible."[12]

Among other ostensible justifications for relegating Burroughs to oblivion, if not banning him entirely,[13] have been his reliance on formulas, belief in Darwinian evolution, inferiority to Kipling, preposterousness, antireligious tendencies and right-wing extremism, excessive violence, infantile appeal,[14] lack of imagination,[15] and snobbery.[16] The list is so general that it fails to distinguish in a meaningful way the quality of Burroughs' writing from that of many other authors. For, beginning with the *Iliad* and moving right on down through the ages and up to the latest bestseller, we would be forced to ban or seriously expurgate most books on the basis of one or another of the suggested criteria.

Probably Burroughs elicits such outrage from even those who have not read his Tarzan novels because some people cannot deal with fantasy, certainly not heroic fantasy. In a perceptive essay, Tom Slate claims that the true objections of the hostile critics revolve primarily around the concept of heroism, around the heroic spirit and its constant effort to raise itself above the mass of men.[17] From Homer's time onward, many a Thersites has raised his envious objections at the mere fact of the heroicness of the hero. An age of institutionalized homogenization is uncomfortable with manifestations of superiority.

There are individual studies that recognize in Burroughs' Tarzan more than a unidimensional figure pandering to the lowest common denominator of the vulgar masses. Dorothy McGreal in a short paper goes so far as to single Tarzan out as perhaps "the only great legendary figure produced by the literature of this century,"[18] and though opinions will surely differ on her assessment, she is correct in placing Tarzan in the tradition of legend and by implication myth. Richard Kyle, in a longer paper from which one of the epigraphs is taken, clearly has a positive view of Burroughs' contribution.[19]

Others have also recognized that there is indeed more to Burroughs than meets the untutored eye. Although no in-depth study exists in English, a work by Richard A. Lupoff deals in part with Tarzan.[20] Lupoff is, however, necessarily brief in his comments on individual books or passages, and his sense of the traditionality of Tarzan as literary creation is largely limited to the immediate context of Burroughs' own age. What is most important about his book is that he does take Burroughs seriously, and for this one should be grateful.

In conclusion, I see Burroughs as a fine artist in his genre of heroic fantasy. His peculiar literary skill is, like Homer's, his ability to combine fantastic and unbelievably exciting adventure stories with commentary on man and his condition. His use of language and literary technique was deeply influenced by his familiarity with the classical languages and literatures, and the discussion of these important facets of his writing in the first two chapters leads into an analysis of the traditional patterns of classical myth and heroic narrative that Burroughs followed. This study, then, hopes to indicate the precise nature of the relationship of Burroughs' Tarzan to the classical prototypes, not because Burroughs needs more readers but because he merits more serious attention than critics and academicians have hitherto given him.

LANGUAGE

___1___

A careful analysis of the Tarzan novels demonstrates the erroneousness of much of the critical thinking about Burroughs' use of language and style. Critics like Seeyle[1] to the contrary, Burroughs' use of repetition and his reliance on formulaic language are not indicia of inferior or uncontrolled writing but rather a measure of his traditionality. The instances of repeated sequences of highly conventional language are numerous in Burroughs' novels as they are in the Homeric epic. (One detailed comparison is given in Appendix I.)

In Homer formal descriptions of warriors dying on the battlefield, the preparation of meals, the beaching of ships, divine councils on Mount Olympus, the reception of strangers, and the mutilation of corpses appear again and again; in Burroughs, the killing of a lion, Tarzan's voicing of a victory cry, swinging through the primeval forest, and the psychological dimension of an entangling and emblematic jungle landscape appear repeatedly.

A detailed investigation of Burroughs' depiction of the jungle demonstrates how he makes the highly traditional feature of epic language, repetition, serve a purpose beyond mere denotative description.

The jungle in the Tarzan novels is often described in a vocabulary that is applicable to the full range of human emotions. Action and thought must occur in some locale, and an author may or may not choose to exploit this necessary element of the narrative. Burroughs does so with considerable sophistication. In itself the jungle is a neutral thing, but Burroughs makes it a moldable symbol. His vocabulary suggests the possibilities of the symbol; context and character define its particular actuality in a given instance. One of the most common verbal clusters that Burroughs uses in constructing his formulas of the jungle entails in some way or another the idea of entanglement, maze-like or labyrinthine involvement, or entwinement. The jungle is a place that ensnares. Consider the following passage.

. . . a small natural amphitheatre which the jungle had left free from its entangling vines and creepers in a hollow among some low hills.
The open space was almost circular in shape. Upon every hand rose the mighty giants of the untouched forest, with the matted undergrowth banked so closely between the huge trunks that the only opening into the little, level arena was through the upper branches of the trees [1.51].

Burroughs is not, of course, merely describing a physical universe. He is also arranging the appropriate backdrop against which human action and motive may be measured—hence, the psychological ambience of the landscape. In this example, the place where the ceremonial dances of the great apes are held is described, for Tarzan here "established his right to respect" (1.51). It was on this occasion and on this spot that Tarzan killed his lifelong enemy and foster father, Tublat. For this reason Burroughs depicts the locale as *free from the entanglements* of the vegetation in the surrounding jungle, and Tarzan is said here to have "won his *emancipation from the persecution* that had followed him remorselessly" (1.52, italics added) for so long. The clearing is where Tarzan establishes his sense of freedom and independence among the tribe of Kerchak; like the passage from the entangling jungle to the level arena, Tarzan's passage from child to man (cf. "man-child" at 1.56) is here initiated, and Kerchak, the king of the tribe, knows it (1.57).

In this example, the physically entangling growth of the jungle serves as an obvious commentary on childhood's emotionally entangling relationships that must be severed. That Tarzan kills his foster father, moreover, is surely not without significance in this little Oedipal drama. (Tublat was, after all, attacking his wife, who was also Tarzan's foster mother, Kala.)

The consistent and cohesive use of a specialized vocabulary in the narrative treatment of this one element, the jungle, suggests its metaphorical and symbolic quality. Since the jungle is the primary arena of dramatic operations, as it were, it is set before the reader with remarkable definition and internal coherence. From the point of view of all but Tarzan (and perhaps his son Korak and daughter-in-law Meriem), the jungle is an essentially negative thing, but one must always keep fresh the awareness that it is not exclusively a place of gloom and gore. The jungle can also appear beautiful (1.3; 4.141; 6.111), luxuriant (3.72), a place of wonders (6.152f.), and even a paradise (2.211).

By means of comfortable and iterative consistency, Burroughs is able to call into being a world that, straddling the manifold uncertainties of the violent jungle and the chaos of civilization, nonetheless comes to be seen as regulated by a definite order. The use of language underscores at every turn the common theme of the possibility for man's imposition of order upon and control over seemingly capricious and random environments. The reader begins to sense the constant juxtaposition of the thing described with the way in which it is described. Very rapidly in the first book, *Tarzan*, the jungle becomes a genuine psychological landscape that both affects and reflects not only the perilous physical activity of human and animal characters, but also their complex and reticulated psychological lives.

In his use of the jungle as psychological landscape, Burroughs displays the same masterful qualities that Homer, Vergil, and Ovid (especially in *The Metamorphoses*) do. In their deployment of descriptive passages of nature and the physical surroundings, they comment on or interpret human actions. Indeed, in much of classical literature one finds this technique exploited to the full, and the above three authors do not exhaust the possibilities. Such descriptive elaborations of locale do not always adumbrate the shadier aspects of human existence and activity but may equally well elucidate the sunlit world of the untrammeled primitive.

Consider the striking blend of psychological externalization and classical allusion that characterizes Burroughs' initial depiction of the jungle at the beginning of the first novel, *Tarzan*. Alice Rutherford and John Clayton, Lord Greystoke, parents-to-be of the jungle-man, are helplessly caught up in the unforeseen and unforeseeable contingencies of a mutiny and are exposed on a savage shore somewhere along the coast of West Africa.

About three o'clock in the afternoon they came about off a beautiful wooded shore opposite the mouth of what appeared to be a landlocked harbor. . . . Before dark the barkentine lay peacefully at anchor upon the bosom of the still, mirror-like surface of the harbor.
The surrounding shores were beautiful with semitropical verdure, while in the distance the country rose from the ocean in hill and table land, almost uniformly clothed by primeval forest [1.13].

This introduction to the world in which the Greystokes will live presents the beneficent side of the jungle, its peaceful qualities, and its unmistakable beauty. Burroughs is at pains, however, to register the real ambivalence of this world. As in all universes created by an author, the physical setting offers a multitude of possibilities.
Many an ancient hero—Achilles was not the first—has discovered that the individual's interior geography is invariably of more significance than the exterior locale, nor has Burroughs neglected to let the reader know of this timeless duality. On the second page we are told, if only in passing, that Greystoke's appointment appalls him because he will have to take his young bride "into the dangers and isolation of tropical Africa." Greystoke himself was worried about being "left to the mercies of savage beasts, and, possibly, more savage men." Furthermore, once dark falls, the land takes on a more sinister character for the principals.

From the dark shadows of the mighty forest came the wild calls of savage beasts—the deep roar of the lion, and, occasionally, the shrill scream of a panther.
The woman shrank closer to the man in terror-stricken anticipation of the horrors lying in wait for them in the awful blackness of the nights to come, when they should be alone upon that wild and lonely shore (1.14].

In these few descriptive passages of the jungle, Burroughs not only establishes with authority the dual nature of the landscape, but also introduces a number of themes or motifs that, with the appropriate verbal elaborations, are woven into the larger context of the universe that he is creating. These themes are not original, but are the common property of Western literary tradition at least from the time of Homer.

Africa—or, more precisely, the jungles of Africa—is characterized as lonely and isolated (1.2, 1.14), and this isolation of the land openly mirrors the utter loneliness of the Greystokes: ". . . now that the horror of absolute solitude was upon them. . ." (1.16). Others will sense the loneliness and isolation of the jungle that the Greystokes have experienced so keenly (for example, William Cecil Clayton, Lord Greystoke, Tarzan's cousin, at 1.112; Jane Porter, realizing that her companion Anderssen will no longer be with her, at 3.93; and the Honorable Morison Baynes at 4.188).

As well as landscape, a second important motif is that of time and its diurnal variations. Night and day, dark and light, and their incessant alternation in the natural world are timeless literary motifs whose provenience extends beyond even Homer. During the early afternoon, the jungle appeared beautiful and nourishing (1.13), but after the coming of "the awful blackness" (1.14) of night, it loomed as a thing more threatening than appealing.

Finally, one may point to the anthropomorphizing metaphor sustained in the initial description of the jungle that the Greystokes encounter (1.13). Their ship comes to the *mouth* of a harbor and lies at anchor on the *bosom* of its waters; the country itself is *clothed* by the forest. The land and its harbor are conceived of as a female entity of both threatening and nurturing potential.

This opening passage of *Tarzan* is reminiscent of a similar landing at the start of Vergil's *Aeneid*. Aenas and his companions have left Troy to found a civilization, and on the way they land at Carthage.

There is a place in a distant bay; an island, its sides lying across the bay, makes a harbor, and all the waves from the open sea break on the sides of the island and split off to the inmost hollows. From both sides huge crags and twin rocks rise menacingly to the sky, and beneath their peaks the surface of the water lies safe and silent. Next, upcountry a background of glittering trees; a dark grove with its bristling shade looms over the scene. Beneath the front of the slope facing the sailors a cave with hanging rocks—within it are sweet waters and abodes of natural stone, home of the nymphs [*Aeneid* I.159–168].

The image is that of the receiving female, and, as it turns out, the female land (*terra*) both nourishes Aeneas and his men and threatens to destroy their enterprise. What they make of the land depends on them. The scene is archetypal.

Both Aeneas and Lord Greystoke come by sea, on their way to "civilize" a new land. (It should be recalled here that Greystoke's mission was to bring English law to the natives of West Africa, and Aenas' was to found Rome.) After a "stormy" trip, they enter a peaceful harbor with luxuriant land, both bright and dark, rising behind it, and they try to set up their "civilization" in this place (both fail).

Burroughs' jungle, then, not only reflects human aspirations and limitations, but, in its ability to sustain or destroy living things itself, it also develops into something almost living and human. The tone has been established at the outset.

Three characteristic features of ancient Greek and Latin style—polarity, chiasmus, and parallelism—are prominent in Burroughs' prose. They apply not only to the use of individual words but also to larger units of discourse such as themes, and we must look at these stylistic phenomena in some detail.

The term polarity has begun to take on pejorative connotations as a result of overuse in political contexts, but as a literary term it refers primarily to the habit of organizing a view of reality into sets of opposites. The perception of reality in the necessarily more comprehensive manner of a double point of view is a hallmark of Greek style. The matter under consideration may be trivial, and the polar statement of it may as a consequence be little more than the reflex operation of a linguistic pattern. At the same time, two points of view are more elucidating (if not always closer to the truth) than one. Polar expressions in a style afford a broader survey and fuller understanding of the person or event described.

To call the human race "men and women" particularizes the concept and therefore views it with greater immediacy; to call the human race "all the Greeks and barbarians" also particularizes the concept, but in a different way. These two examples, both of which are very common in Greek literature, show that polar expressions can strongly influence the way an audience views a given phenomenon. The phrase "daily life," for instance, is not very illuminating, but if we use a polar phrase to describe the same thing we can greatly affect perceptions of the item described. Such terms as the "daily agony and ecstasy," "daily work and relaxation," "daily bread and drink," "daily thought and action," and any number of others all describe the basic idea "daily life," but each attaches quite distinct and different meanings to the general term.

Burroughs delights in the polar view of the world that he creates, and this polar outlook permeates his handling of themes. Tarzan's father, John Clayton, receives his commission to go to Africa to untangle a diplomatic difficulty, and "he was both elated and appalled" (1.2). The polar expression (which particularizes the "mixed emotions" of the man) helps to characterize Clayton, for it serves as the basis of the immediately following elaboration of the commission as a promotion for his career and a setback for his wife's well-being. Clayton is dealt with fully in the opening of the work despite his death not many pages later, for he is that noble ideal (in 1912) of civilized maleness whose genetic influence will over many years be constantly present in the offspring, Tarzan. This concern for the private world of his wife and the public domain of his career and country is itself part of the characterization of Tarzan's father, and it follows the classical biographical precedent of always dealing with a man in his capacity as a public servant and a private member of his own family. The use of the polar expression here provides the springboard for viewing Clayton with a fullness that a less pleonastic phrasing might have rendered difficult.

One of the informing polarities in the world of Tarzan is that of man and animal, especially man and ape, and in the course of the books a Darwinian synthesis emerges from this ongoing dialectic.

This polarity appears frequently in some form, including man and ape (1.84), civilized man and jungle folk (3.22), Korak the human and Akut the ape (4.63), and woman and female ape (6.158).

The diurnal rhythms of the jungle world and its inhabitants are commonly expressed by the polarity of day and night. Thus, at 3.26 Tarzan's existence in the jungle is seen against the backdrop of stalking beasts and imminent threats "by savage day or by cruel night." Korak's first time in the jungle after escaping with Akut is described as follows: "That night the son of Tarzan was colder than he ever had been in all his life. . . . And the next day he roasted in the hot sun . . ." (4.50). When the evil Rokoff is trying to extricate himself from his unpleasant predicament in the jungle, he flees "the hideous horde racing after him by day and by night, now abreast of him, now lost in the mazes of the jungle far behind. . ." (3.112). On the next page we find once more the "hideous days and nights" and "long days and weary nights." In *Son*, the lions "ranged the plains and hills by night, or laid up in the cool wood by day" (4.149). And at the beginning of *Tarzan*, it will be recalled, the introduction of the Claytons to the jungle took place during the brightness of afternoon and the gloom of dusk (1.13f.).

These few examples make clear some additional features of polar expression. One polar phrase may attract another into its sphere, so to speak, in the way that night and day here also become poles on which to hang the contrasts of cold and heat (4.50), of keeping up and falling behind (3.112), of ranging in the open and lying in the wood (4.149), and, in the last example, of the implicit warmth set against the cool.

Such accumulations of polar expressions are nicely illustrated in a passage from *Tales*. Tarzan has just kidnapped a young boy, Tibo, whom he wants to make into his own *balu* (child).

He would tend him carefully, feed him well, protect him as only Tarzan of the Apes could protect his own, and teach him out of his half human, half bestial lore the secrets of the jungle from its rotting surface vegetation to the high tossed pinnacles of the forest's upper terraces [6.70].

Several polarities underlie this passage and arrange it into an ordered whole. The ideas of tend, feed, and protect speak to the physical well-being of Tibo, and teaching him involves his mental or intellectual well-being. The polarity that is basic here is that of body-mind, one of the more prevalent ones in ancient literature in the description of men. Tarzan, in other words, is going to make of his child a whole man. Tarzan's own qualifications for carrying out this project rest on his dual background as human and beast, and therefore he can teach the youth the best from both worlds. Finally, what he will teach is itself polarized in the rather common vertical formulation that Burroughs likes (cf. 1.207: "pinnacle of hope . . . utter depths of despair"). "surface vegetation" and "high tossed pinnacles." All three sets of polar underpinnings are elaborate ways to universalize, for Tibo will be made into a complete man, he will be taught from all traditions, and he will be taught all aspects of the jungle. The use of polarized language in this passage would have been very familiar to an ancient Greek, whose language was itself inherently polar in both conception and expression.

The polarity of genetics-environment, which becomes one of the more basic themes in Burroughs, is deftly stated at 1.139.

Tarzan of the Apes had a man's figure and a man's brain, but he was an ape by training and environment. His brain told him that the chest contained something valuable . . . his training had taught him to imitate whatever was new and unusual.

The contrasting polarities of dream-reality (2.153, 2.212, 6.134) and memory-reality (4.131) are used several times in Burroughs, and so are those of pleasure-sorrow (3.13), hunters-tillers (3.49), man-made town—God-made jungle (4.31), fabulous rewards-condign punishment (3.136), native-white (4.168), war-peace (5.32), past-future (5.64), and many more. Indeed, many of the notions that interest Burroughs are in origin simple polarities elevated to the more complex role of theme.

Chiasmus, the second basic feature of both Greek and Latin style, is more at home in a highly inflected language like Greek or Latin than in less synthetic ones like English. It is , however, found in English, too. At its simplest, a chiasmus is an arrangement of four words in such a way that A is to B as B is to A. The As and the Bs may be adjectives, nouns, verbs, words for sitting, standing, doing, or any other set of terms that share some common principle or characteristic. Alexander Pope was very fond of this device (probably because of his extensive readings in and translations of classical authors),as is shown in the following example:

Sylvia's like autumn ripe, yet mild as May.

Here the framing words "autumn" and "May" refer to seasons, and the central words "ripe" and "mild" mention qualities, or

season : quality :: quality : season
(A)   (B)   (B)   (A)

The device is no doubt a convenient means for organizing bits of information into a coherent structure that will select the related items and make comprehension of them easy. It may seem an obvious thing to do in the case of the four words cited above, but this principle of chiasmus has much more important applications in other contexts than the exclusively verbal one. Chiasmus is at any rate endemic to both Greek and Latin style, neither of which is imaginable in their developed states without it. It occurs in modern English but is not common; Burroughs' use of it in the restricted application to sets of two words each can be quite striking.

In a dramatic scene at 1.61, for example, Tarzan wishes to test his new discovery that a rope can be used to catch animals. He recently had an unfortunate experience with a boar he had tried to rope, and he realized that a larger animal would have killed him because of his inexperience. Now, however, he is going to try the rope out on a larger animal, Sabor the lioness: "Like a thing of bronze, motionless as death, sat Tarzan. Sabor passed beneath." The chiasmus is obvious (sat : Tarzan :: Sabor : passed). It is very compact, for there are no invervening words or phrases to break up the perfect structure. It should also be noted that chiasmus, as in this example, often lends itself to contrasts of the type we examined in connection with polar expressions. Here, for instance, we have the underlying polarities of rest-motion (sat-passed) and man-animal (Tarzan-Sabor), and the chiastic arrangement creates a certain tension in the placement of the opposition; it is as though the physical placement of the words on the page underscore the opposition or confrontation between Tarzan and Sabor.

To what does the adverbial modification "beneath" in the second half of the sentence correspond? The word in a most general sense more closely defines the idea "Sabor passed," and in the same general way in the first half of the sentence, the phrase "like a thing of bronze, motionless as death" modifies the idea in "sat Tarzan." Grammatically, the first part of the first sentence is a prepositional phrase, and the last part of the second is adverbial. Both, however, are identical in that each modifies its respective subject and verb. Looked at as an expanded chiastic structure, the whole sentence may, then, be analyzed as

A (modifiers)
B (verb)
C (subject)
C (subject)
B (verb)
A (modifier)

That the modifiers are of disparate complexity is irrelevant to the organization, if not the sense, of the sentence. From this discussion it may be extrapolated that no intrinsic reason exists for limiting such a structure to three sets of terms, and in fact many more may be employed.

At 4.67 Korak and Akut have come upon a band of apes who are celebrating the rites of the Dum-Dum and are waiting until the excitement dies down before making themselves known to the enraptured celebrants.

As the moon declined slowly toward the lofty, foliaged horizon of the amphitheatre the *booming* of the drum *decreased* and *lessened were* the *exertions* of the dancers, *until*, at last, the final note was struck and the huge beasts turned to fall upon the feast they had dragged hither for the orgy. [Italics added]

A very simple chiasmus here provides the organizing impetus for a very balanced rhythmic sentence consisting of two sets, subjects ("booming" and "exertions") and verbs ("decreased" and "lessened were"), arranged as follows:

booming : decreased : : lessened : exertions.

In this instance, however, the chiasmus has none of the compactness seen in the previous one, for the framing chiastic terms are themselves embellished in somewhat balanced phrasings,

> the booming of the drum
> the exertions of the dancers.

It may be noted first that, rather than being polar, the chiasmus is glossing, for both terms refer to a diminution of unusual activity. Furthermore, the chiastic core of four terms is itself flanked by two subordinate clauses, both temporal, so that there is an expanded chiastic arrangement. These subordinations reflect from the natural world (moon, apes) the dominant idea (diminution) of the chiastic core of the sentence, for in the description of the moon's "decline" and the animals' "falling upon" we have reiteration of the central notion at the physical level. It coheres internally because the component parts of it speak to and comment on each other in constant reinforcement.

Also direct is the more complex chiasmus at 6.65. A young ape's distractibility from more serious pursuits is being discussed: ". . . the *caterpillars* he *always* caught, and *sometimes* the *beetles*; but the field *mice, never.*"

A passage at 4.220 demonstrates the potential for expressions that is inherent in any chiastic combination: "The man's story led the Admiral to believe that the place where the white girl the Arab supposed to be my daughter was held in captivity was not far from your African estates . . . and he advised that . . ." The chiasmus in this passage is of a different order from the examples examined above. There each chiasmus was one of verbal elements; here it is a grammatical one. The point that needs emphasis, however, is that in all the examples the underlying principle that organizes the whole is chiasmus. Of interest to us in the citation is the entire subordinate clause introduced by "believe that." On the basis of its own subordinated structure it is organized in the following fashion.

| Main | the place . . . was not far |
| Clause | from your African estates |

First Degree of Subordination	where the white girl . . . was held in captivity
Second Degree of Subordination	(whom) the Arab supposed to be my daughter

If we assign As to the main clause (of what is itself a subordinate clause in the larger sentence), Bs to the first degree of subordination, and C to the second degree of subordination, the arrangement based on syntactic disposition is

$$A \; : \; B \; : \; C \; : \; B \; : \; A$$

The C is apparently intrusive in the chiastic structure and is unlike anything we have noted up to this point. In fact, however, the use of C here points up an extremely important extension of chiasmus, in which framing elements (such as As, Bs) quite literally and physically encompass a central element and focus the attention on what is contained within the borders of the surrounding frame. In this instance, attention is indeed directed to the central element, the C , which states "(whom) the Arab supposed to be my daughter."

The search of children for maturity and of parents for their lost children are central themes of *Son*, a kind of Telemacheia, and the speaker of the lines above is General Armand Jacot. His daughter was kidnapped by Arabs long ago, and only now, at the very end of the child's wanderings (along with the parallel thematic development of Korak's wanderings), does the father at last rediscover the waif, who is Meriem. The centrality of the theme and the importance of the imminent *anagnorisis*, or recognition, of each other by father and daughter are underlined by the stylistic manipulation which places the phrase about the supposed daughter in the center of the surrounding frame. Thus, the phrasings of the language inform semantically at a supralexical level by their very arrangement in physical space. This procedure is quite classical in its architectonic design. The entire *Iliad* of Homer, to mention but one work, is a vast and complex collocation of some 15,000 lines of poetry organized into a unified whole largely through the constant and unerring operation of chiasmus.

The psychological antithesis and hostility between the wily Arab, Achmet Zek, and the renegade Belgian, Werper, is cast in sharp relief by the chiastic style at 5.10: "*Achmet Zek* scowled and *Werper's* heart sank; but *Werper* did not know *Achmet Zek*, who was quite apt to *scowl* where another would *smile*, and *smile* where another would *scowl*" (italics added). The plaited language mirrors the tangled suspicions which these two villains feel for each other at the opening of the book and continue to harbor until, in a scene of deepest mistrust and sustained hatred, Werper finally kills the Arab (5.122). Two sets of chiasmus organize the sentence and underscore the extreme ambivalence of the two men toward each other in this malevolent confrontation.

1. Achmet Zek : Werper : : Werper : Achmet Zek
2. scowl : smile : : smile : scowl

The third major feature of Greek and Latin style is what may be thought of as the complement of chiasmus, parallelism. Parallelism is no doubt more comfortable a mode in English than chiasmus, and it appears more commonly than initial impressions may suggest. If chiasmus consists of the arrangement

$$A : B :: B : A$$

parallelism by contrast is the structure

$$A : B :: A : B.$$

Parallelism is at work in this line from Alexander Pope's *Spring*.

In spring the fields, in autumn hills I love
(A) : (B) : : (A) : (B)

This stylistic feature is quite common in Burroughs. As with chiasmus, parallelism is not to be considered mere stylistic puffery, but as one of many ways an author may highlight or emphasize a given word, motif, or passage. In addition, skillful use of parallelism, much like that of chiasmus, may depict physically on the page aspects of the action that the language describes.

At a dramatic juncture in *Tarzan*, the hero kills a lioness and as a result saves the life of Jane and his cousin, John. "Higher crept the steel forearms of the apeman about the back of Sabor's neck. Weaker and weaker became the lioness' efforts" (1.121). The word order of the first sentence is accurately duplicated in the second.

A	(comparative adjective predicated of the subject)	higher
	B (verb)	crept
	C (subject with modifiers)	the steel forearms of the apeman
A		weaker and weaker
	B	became
	C	the lioness' efforts

The odd phrase is "about the back of Sabor's neck," and its central importance in the parallel structure is emphasized by its central position. Caught between the steely power of Tarzan and her own growing weakness, the lioness can only die. Moreover, the wedding of beast and Tarzan in mortal struggle is suggested by the overall parallelism of the language, for the words duplicate the parallel movements of the man in his conquest of the animal. Burroughs makes the words work for him not only as specific semantic indicators but also as commentary on the meaning of the unified whole.

It is now time to consider in greater detail how Burroughs puts his sentences together. Here, too, it will become obvious that he is not the careless writer of popular critical fancy but rather has a remarkably accurate sense of how language can underscore or undercut the psychology of characters or add to the internal drive of the narrative.

In an analysis of Burroughs' style, it seems appropriate to begin with the first paragraph of *Tarzan*.

I had this story from one who had no business to tell it to me, or to any other. I may credit the seductive influence of an old vintage upon the narrator for the beginning of it, and my own skeptical incredulity during the days that followed for the balance of the strange tale.

This opening statement displays considerable stylistic sophistication. It consists of two sentences, both of which begin with the same subject ("I") followed immediately by a main verb ("had" and "may credit") and end with its complementing predications. These latter deserve closer scrutiny.

In sentence one we have the following.

```
                                                      to me
this story from one who had no business to tell it      or
                                                      to any other
```

In the second sentence we find:

```
                    the seductive influence
                    of an old vintage

                        upon the narrator

                            for the beginning
                            of it

            and

                    my own skeptical
                    incredulity

                        during the days
                        that followed

                            for the balance of
                            the strange tale
```

This organization is clearly parallel, and a number of additional features enhance the coherence of the whole.

Phonic echos may be noted in "SEductive INfluence" and "SkEptical INcredulity," as well as in "FOR THE BEginning OF" and "FOR THE BAlance OF." Prepositional markers set off the grouped phrasings in "upon" and "during," and also in the duplicated "for." The concluding contrast of "beginning" and "balance" in sentence two mirrors the concluding contrast of "me" and "any other" in the first sentence.

It is useless—and in my view frivolous—to speculate whether this construction was the result of conscious intent. The incontrovertible fact is that Burroughs' opening paragraph is written in the way in which we have it. It reflects a way he thought and conceptualized, and it does yield to the type of analysis undertaken here. The strongly polar construction of the paragraph may well stand as emblematic of the polar view which Burroughs imposes on the world of his creation. It may be argued that not one reader in a hundred would catch the stylistic sophistication in this first paragraph, and that is possibly true. The point is, however, that an author's stylistic patterns (like thematic and narrative patterns) that are frequently iterated create an expectation, no matter how subliminal, that the author must satisfy if he is to continue to involve his reader.

An interestingly developed sentence occurs at 6.13. A young she-ape, Teeka, pursued by a leopard, is rescued by Tarzan.

And just as Teeka sprang for the lower limb of a great tree, and Sheeta rose behind her in a long, sinuous leap, the coils of the ape-boy's grass rope shot swiftly through the air, straightening into a long thin line as the open noose hovered for an instant above the savage head and the snarling jaws.

The main sentence ("the coils . . . the air") is comfortably tucked in between two surrounding subordinations that are of approximately equal length. The subordinations are varied in that the one at the beginning of the sentence takes the form of two temporal clauses (introduced by "as"), but the one at the end is a participial modifier ("straightening") with its own subordination ("as the noose . . ."). Consider the opening first.

> And just as
>> Teeka sprang for the lower limb of a great tree
> and
>> Sheeta rose behind her in a long, sinuous leap.

The first part contains twelve syllables, the second has thirteen. There is a certain play in the opening names (Teeka-Sheeta) with their parallel vowel sequences (ee-a), and it perhaps alerts the reader familiar with stylistic conventions to the possibilities that may follow. Each subject is followed by its verb of upward motion ("sprang," "rose"), which in turn is more closely defined by modifiers that in both phrases are prefaced by prepositions ("for," and "behind," and "in"). The two coordinations are quite parallel in their organization, and present the polar viewpoint of hunted and hunter, a favorite polarity in Burroughs' works, and one which here is shortly inverted when hunter Sheeta becomes hunted by Tarzan. The present participle "straightening," which introduces the closing phrase, has the same time as the two verbal ideas in the opening, introduced by temporal "as," and itself ushers in a concluding temporal as-clause ("as the open noose . . .") in balance to the opening ones. Moreover, the final part is split into two (alliterative: SAVAJ-SNA-JA) phrases.

> the *savage* head
> . . . above   and
> the *sn*arling *ja*ws

This bifurcation at the end also balances the bifurcation of as-clauses in the beginning of the sentence. Central to this little drama of hunter and hunted is Tarzan with his rope, for with his rope he rescues the she-ape. And, as one might expect, the centrality of his role in this sentence is emphasized by physical placement of the section that deals with him.

Another example of Burroughs' style that at first reading may appear too complicated grammatically, and therefore clumsy, comes at 5.37. Tarzan has just regained consciousness after having lain in a coma as a result of a cave-in. He is trying to find his way out of the dark chambers that lie beneath the city of Opar, and at one point in the search he has reached the stairway at the end of a passage.

It turned back and forth many times, leading, at last, into a smaller, circular chamber, the gloom of which was relieved by a faint light which found ingress through a tubular shaft several feet in diameter which rose from the center of the room's ceiling, upward to a distance of a hundred feet or more, where it terminated in a stone grating through which Tarzan could see a blue and sun-lit sky.

This prose is hardly elegant, but does this apparent deficiency stem from carelessness in composition, or does the strained style attempt to say something over and beyond the denotation of the words? Consider the sentence in closer detail.

Grammatically, it concludes in the first line at "times;" in sense, it perhaps extends through the particular modification "leading . . . chamber." Everything from "the gloom" to the end is appended as a very weak relative clause introduced by "of which." This relative clause is itself inordinately involuted in its structure. The skeleton is indicated in the following outline.

Main sentence
1.   the gloom of WHICH was . . . by a faint light
2.   WHICH found . . . shaft
3.   WHICH rose . . .
4.   WHERE it terminated . . . grating
5.   through WHICH *Tarzan* . . . sky.

The first relative clause introduces a first degree of subordination, the second relative a second degree, and so on through the fifth one (note that "where" in number four introduces a relative, not an adverbial, clause). It is of crucial importance to recognize that these relatives are *not* coordinated relatives, but subordinated. For the relatives are not of the same degree, all subordinated to "chamber. Rather, there is an increasing removal through successive subordinations of degree from the main clause, until, at the final subordination, the main clause is five degrees removed. This structure of cascading subordinations is indeed extraordinary and generally more than normal English can carry. If nothing else, it must surely catch the reader's attention by its very oddity.

The plot of *Jewels* is among other things concerned with the search for a pouch of jewels, the jewels being symbolic of identity. This tale is the classical one of the search for self, and the process begins in the passage we are discussing. Dead to the world, as it were, from the blow in the subterranean chamber that has just rendered him unconscious, Tarzan and his past have been buried alive in the treasure vaults of Opar. Tarzan can only move up; he can only search for and regain his lost identity.

In view of this thematic setting of the involuted sentence beginning with the stairway that "turned back and forth many times," it now becomes possible at least to suggest some of the implications of the reticulated structure of the language. It will be recalled that it is in the final subordination, at the farthest grammatical remove from the main sentence, that the name of Tarzan appears. Quite literally, Tarzan is at this point as far removed from knowledge of himself and who he is as the degree of subordination is from the main sentence. The stairway is itself symbolic of the ascent that must be made, and the entire notion of rising from a nothing or nobody is here closely allied to Burroughs' views on Darwinism and the rise of man from primitive beginnings (cf. later at 5.37: "Tarzan, reverted to the primitive by the accident . . ."). The immediate point is simply that the cumbersome sentence can be read as purposefully cumbersome because its very structure says at least as much, if not more, about the major theme of the book as do the individual words. Style, then, and, in this case, a grammatical organization that may at first glance appear clumsy prove on more detailed inspection to display considerable functional elegance.

Pleasing style need not, of course, always exist for ulterior purposes of underscoring or undercutting the meaning that denotations of words convey. It may simply be a pleasing thing in its own right, a part of the totality of impressions that makes an author that particular author and not another. In any one instance, the style could be changed or even eliminated without affecting the larger work. Too much tampering, however, would eventually result in something quite different from the original.

The following paragraph is a delightful piece of writing. It is straightforward, descriptive, and classical in its movement. The ape

Chulk has come upon the sleeping Mugambi and has decided to take the latter's knobstick and pouch.

Seizing these two articles, as better than nothing at all, Chulk retreated with haste, and every indication of nervous terror, to the safety of the tree from which he had dropped, and still haunted by that indefinable terror which the close proximity of man awakened in his breast, fled precipitately through the jungle. Aroused by attack, or supported by the presence of another of his kind, Chulk could have braved the presence of a score of human beings, but alone—ah, that was a different matter—alone, and unenraged [5.116].

The two sentences offer a splendid example of the three basic features of ancient style that we have been treating. The first sentence is arranged as a parallel structure, the second is a chiasmus, and the basic polarity of retreat-attack informs the whole. Let us examine the passage more closely.

The first sentence is compound, each half being itself complex; the parallelism of the structure is worked out exactingly.

> General
> A   (participial phrase)
> B   (subject)
> C   (verb)
> D   (verbal modifiers)

> Specific
> A Seizing these . . . nothing at all
>   B Chulk
>   C retreated
>   D with haste . . . had dropped

> A still haunted . . . in his breast
>   B (Chulk)
>   C fled
>   D precipitately through the jungle

In a change of stylistic pace, then, the second sentence inverts the parallel structure of the first sentence and appears as a chiasmus.

A Aroused by attack
  B or supported by the presence of another of his kind
    C Chulk could have braved the presence of a score
      of human beings
  B but alone—ah, that was a different matter—alone
A and unenraged.

The As and Bs function antithetically. In the As, a contrast is set up between "aroused by attack" and "unenraged," which is to say that to be enraged is to be aroused by attack and vice versa; in the Bs, the contrast is between many and one. Hence, the stylistic patterns that these two sentences reveal could easily have been lifted from the pages of a host of classical authors.

The two sentences themselves, it should be noted, are cast as one biological, archetypal polarity—flight-fight—which, in conjunction with the happy style, perhaps accounts for the satisfying echoes that the paragraph creates. Who of us, for all our human sophistication, has not on some occasions felt "that indefinable terror which the close proximity of man awakened?" To confront or back down?

Harmonious style need not rely on complex subordinations. This was not always the case among the ancient writers, nor, quite certainly, is it the case with Burroughs. Simple coordination may work equally well, and to avoid leaving the impression that Burroughs embroiled himself in an exclusively complex sentence structure, I may cite the following passage. Tarzan, imprisoned in the hold of a ship on which he believes he will find his kidnapped son, searches for an exit: "To this end he examined his prison carefully, tested the heavy planking that formed its walls, and measured the distance of the hatch above him" (3.13). Not a whisper of subordination here, but the sentence works very well. Once past the introductory "To this end he," we find three parallel noncomplex parts set up in a very clear pattern.

VERB	OBJECT	MODIFIER
examined	his prison	carefully
tested	the heavy planking	that formed its walls
measured	the distance	of the hatch above him

The verbs are all synonymous; the objects are vaguely similar in that they all refer to aspects of the prison; only the modifiers deviate somewhat, for the first modifies the verb, and the others, the object. The sentence moves from a generalization in the first part to an increasingly more specific reformulation of the opening. Here we get three points of view about the event described, and the calm dignity of the language is a measured reflection of the competent and un-hysterical search Tarzan undertakes.

For all of Burroughs' considerable skill in handling the language, however, his prose is not always deathless. There are examples of so-called purple prose, of the stylistic attempt that overreaches itself and degenerates into a kind of artless and unintentionally (one presumes) amusing use of language. One may easily castigate Burroughs and "prove" that he was a dreadful writer if one cites the appropriate passages. The truth, I think, lies somewhere between the extremes. He has very fine moments as a stylist, and he has less fortunate ones. He is therefore in excellent company.

A brief look at the history of post-Homeric Greek literature, at its subsequent expropriation by Latin authors, and at Burroughs' education, will suggest a genuine relationship between Burroughs' style and that of heroic poetry.

Whether or not the Greek poets of a later day approved of Homer (and some did not), they were inextricably bound up in Homer's thought, language, and phraseology. Homer was to a large part *the* education of the Greeks, and his two poems, the *Iliad* and the *Odyssey*, were held in the highest esteem by the majority of the Greeks. From Homer one learned the codes of behavior, the appropriate action in the given circumstance, all the known and unknown assumptions that made or did not make the society func-tion. In short, Homer was Greek *paideia*, Greek education, culture, and upbringing.

Post-Homeric poets continued to use the same vocabulary and phraseology as Homer had. Like the poets, the prose writers were brought up on Homer, and although they turned to a different form of discourse to express their ideas, the stamp of Homeric technique, if not always of Homeric language, is everywhere evident. With the possible exception of a more "epic" writer of history like Herodotus, historians, orators, and philosophers of the fifth and fourth centuries B.C. drew on a somewhat different vocabulary from that of Homer, but the stylistic devices and narrative techniques they relied on were found already in Homer's poetry. Therefore, an indisputable continuity of the Homeric tradition can be found in all post-Homeric literature.

By the third century, however, the age-old forms began to grow tired and lose some of their vigor. At that point, Greek literature was given a critical infusion of fresh, young, and bold ideas by the Latin-speaking peoples of the Italian peninsula. These people, in their strong though not universal enthusiasm for all things Greek, provide a crucial link not only in the preservation of the Greek literary tradition, but also in its elaboration and further growth.

The great epics of Homer, like so much else of Greek literature, exercised a profound influence on the language, themes, and thought of Roman literature. Indeed, what is generally agreed to be the crowning achievement of Latin literature, Vergil's *Aeneid*, is unthinkable without the Homeric prototypes. It is a cliché of Vergilian criticism to observe that Vergil's *Aeneid* is based in the first six books on Homer's *Odyssey*, and in the last six, on Homer's *Iliad*. Nor, it must be understood, is this in any sense to suggest that Vergil "copied" Homer or was inferior to Homer, for in its very different way Vergil's epic, drawing on an established tradition first known from Homer, is surely an equally fine poem. It is quite impossible to deny that Vergil constantly had Homer before his mind's eye as he wrote the *Aeneid* during a ten-year period (29–19 B.C.). The language (though Latin rather than Homeric Greek), the themes, the narrative techniques all leave the matter beyond dispute. Yet, Vergil created something totally different from Homer's poem, despite the fact that he drew so heavily on Homer and other Greek writers who themselves were in a more direct line of descent from Homer than Vergil was.

It is most directly from the Romans and their literature rather than from the Greeks that the traditions of Western literature derive. Ultimately, of course, it is to the Greeks that we must return, but our literature, be it "great" or "popular," is unthinkable without the vital and vitalizing mediation of the Romans.

This briefest of sketches, illustrating the main lines of the relationship among Greek, Latin, and modern literature, is clearly not complete, but it suffices as background for a portrait of the origin of Burroughs' style.

Irwin Porges' biography of Burroughs provides an authoritative source for Burroughs' younger years and his education.[2] For it is from Burroughs' studies and early reading that the seeds must have been sown, not only for the ideas and themes with which he was obsessed but also for the particulars of the language, style and narrative technique he came to use. As a youth, Burroughs had difficulties in school and as a result was shunted about from one institution to another. He does not appear to have been particularly fond of school or the subjects he had to study, but, like most students in the high schools of the day, he did study Latin. We also know that during the apparently unhappy period at Phillips Academy in 1891–1892, he studied Greek. It is not clear if Burroughs studied more than first-year Greek at Phillips, but since he had already studied Greek at the Harvard School in Chicago before being sent to Phillips, it is not unlikely that he in fact did some Homer in Greek. It is clear, however, that Burroughs was quite a Latin student, for by his own admission he devoted some eight years to the language. He read, among other authors, parts of Ovid and Vergil's *Aeneid* but above all from the *Commentaries* of Julius Caesar.[3]

As a writer, Caesar was very much in the Roman historiographical tradition, whose origin, like so much else Roman, was Greek. In Caesar's *Commentaries,* one finds many of the tendencies in the use of language and style that appear, *mutatis mutandis*, in other Roman historians and their Greek predecessors. For Caesar, like all writers of antiquity, resorted to the use of set vocabulary to depict given scenes in his work. Composing the *Commentaries* very much like a dramatic narrative, Caesar employed the devices of the narrative artist, such as elaborate rhetoric, repetitive vocabulary, and recurring elements of discourse.

Through inadvertence or a natural penchant from the English point of view to avoid repetition of the same or similar vocabulary, a translator of Caesar may well fail to bring these stylistic traits across into English. But they are present in the original, and after a while the reader accepts them and even expects them. Burroughs, having studied Latin for eight years, was no novice in the language and, simply by having read Caesar (and other Latin authors, who in their fashion do much the same thing), must have absorbed these features of the style. If he did in fact also read Homer and other Greeks authors in Greek, he could not have failed to take cognizance of the repetitions, for Homer is much more repetitive (in the sense shown in Appendix I) than any other ancient author.

What I am suggesting, then, is that Burroughs relies greatly on clusters of similar vocabulary and the stylistic patterns we have examined because, consciously or not, he is following the model of those classical authors whom he read in Latin and, to a lesser and more uncertain extent, Greek. It would be very nice to know that Burroughs consciously decided to emulate Homer's heroic language in devising a world and life for his own great hero, but to my knowledge there is no explicit evidence for this suggestion. One may at any rate observe that Burroughs' youngest son, John Coleman Burroughs, noted as late as 1970 that "his father's style of writing had been strongly influenced by the Latin studies of his early school years."[4] Burroughs himself was "willing to concede that imagination is stimulated by what one reads, but he understood that beyond this, the creative process worked in mysterious ways that often defied analysis."[5]

The contention that Burroughs' style is based ultimately on Homeric Greek finds further suppport in the discussion of technique rather than language alone, for here, too, Burroughs is not unlike Homer and other ancient writers. From an early age, Burroughs had a strong interest in Greece and Greek mythology and in Rome and her legends. In fact, he even turned to mythology and Latin vocabulary as an aid in devising names for the hundreds of characters in his novels.[6]

In his characteristic use of repetitive language, Burroughs compellingly echoes the heroic worlds of an earlier literature. The worlds in which Homer's heroes move are contingent ones. Death may come at any moment, treachery is always near, the certainties of peacetime vanish in the turmoil of war, enemies become friends, the prospect of slavery is never distant for women and children, human relationships are fragile, and the divine world appears to involve itself in the human one on personal whim alone. In brief, the world Homer describes is one of real dissolution and moral ambiguity in which men must try to find some sort of permanence or fixed pattern for the living of their lives. The poet's language depicts a chaotic world in which few, if any, human beings fully understand the ground rules of behavior. (The violation of various codes is a persistent theme of the poems.) This disjointed universe is at the same time described in a highly ordered metrical pattern with language that is predictably regular and consistent in its repetitiveness. While the language itself reflects a supreme orderliness and stability, it also describes a world that is being torn apart. The language always holds before the listener the availability of an order, the possibility of change from the present chaos to a future harmony. For an audience there is surely as deeply felt a satisfaction in the short verbal formulas that are repeated endlessly as in the long scenes with their parade of expected and anticipated motifs, for these recurring passages are the stable points of reference in the ceaseless and often conflicting tides of human action and motivation. They are anchoring grounds.

What kind of world does Burroughs envision for his hero and his villains? The topography is basically tripartite: the land of nature (jungle and desert), the sea, and the land of civilization (cities). All three in their own way are cruel, capricious, and fraught with danger. And here, again, the language, especially that of the jungle, is regularized to an astonishing degree; the jungle is a confusing and chaotic tangle of ensnaring creepers and vines, yet it is described in a vocabulary that becomes established throughout the novels. Little effort is made to vary these descriptions, and the regularity itself is not without its comforting and stabilizing suggestions: men and animals may in their unpredictability behave in beastly or noble fashion, but the jungle somehow abides, a merciless if neutral and stable presence. Like its language, it is basically predictable. The description of the jungle is, of course, not the only set passage, nor is the vocabulary that clusters around it the only group of repeated words. All such passages, no matter how chaotic and hazardous the event or scene described, inject the all-important note of regularity. In the dangerous world of Tarzan, there is in fact a discernible order, and it emerges partially from the language and its style.

I do not view an author's style as a means for prettifying, as something extrinsic that can be excised from the content. Style, in language as in other spheres, springs from the deepest layers of one's personality and vision of the world, and one will indeed try to copy, adopt, and adapt the style of others who have gone before. This we all do to some extent. If it fits, fine; but no person can, in the long run, live with a style, be it of language, dress, or any other external manifestation, that is not consistent with an inner reality. Burroughs did not dream up his style, but he acquired it both from his study of classical languages and literature and from his reading in authors who shared that tradition. Because the style fit, he used it and developed it along his own particular lines, to work for his own particular ends; its roots in the Graeco-Roman tradition are, however, ineradicable.

Burroughs himself was deeply suspicious of style, associating it with literature as defined by the academicians and critics. His own view was that "each writer had his own method of expressing himself—his style"[7] but that style was not something one consciously strove for. It was a part of the writer.

In general, Burroughs seems to have denigrated his own works as literature, insisting at one time that he wrote only to entertain and never to instruct and admitting at another time that his stories "might carry a beneficial suggestion of the value of physical perfection and morality."[8] This dual explanation is in fact lifted straight out of the classical tradition in Western literature, namely, that literature must do two things, entertain and delight (*delectare*) as well as instruct and teach (*docere*). Burroughs belongs to this tradition.

Much of his apparent disparagement[9] of the novels was defensive, and the postured indifference was perhaps in no small part meant to deflate critics and the consistently hostile and nasty comments made about his works by the intellectuals in the universities.[10]

Regardless of whether he knew it or not, Burroughs did have a very sensitively developed feeling for classical style and the things it can do, and his training in the classical languages must be seen as largely responsible for this feeling. On this important point, then, I must take exception to Porges' analysis of Burroughs as a stylist. He seems to have been convinced by Burroughs' own protestations, for he claims that the use of style for "a psychological probing of characters or a perception of social issues" (precisely the sort of thing demonstrated, for example, on the "stairway" passage at 5.37) "were beyond Burroughs' scope."[11] Everybody seems to have been swayed by Burroughs' self-deprecation and by the common "knowledge" that he knew nothing about style.[12] Therefore, no one has bothered to undertake the detailed stylistic analysis performed here. While I have examined only a few passages, an analysis of every sentence obviously being impractical, they are indicative. The reader, once made aware of the workings of Burroughs' stylistic mind, will have no problems finding numerous examples for his own dissection and pondering.

Having given my technical reasons for lingering over these devices of language and repetition in Burroughs' novels, I conclude this chapter with an aesthetic point. Clever or sophisticated use of language for clever or sophisticated reasons is, on a sustained basis, insufficient justification for its existence. Language must always be an organically integrated element of a work of literature, and not something that leaves behind the original, merely missing its distinctive language. For despite its occasional lapses into ungrammatical, stylistically unhappy and inflated prose, the language of Burroughs' novels far more commonly proves at an ultradenotational level to be an incisive commentary on the psychology of characters, the symbolic dimensions of locale, and the interior momentum of action. In both the successful exercise of the potential niceties of language and in the less fortunate slips, Burroughs shows himself to be squarely in the long tradition of that heroic literature that stretches back to the worlds of Vergil's dutiful Aeneas, Homer's adventuresome Odysseus and sulking Achilles, and all the authorless superbeings of ancient myth and legend.

TECHNIQUE

2

If language deals with organization at the most elementary level of the arrangement of words, technique deals with the organization of themes and motifs as expressed in language. And just as the collocation of words, by virtue of physical location in a sentence, can say more about meaning than the sum of their denotations, so the physical location of themes and motifs comment on and interpret both character and action over and above the explicit formulations.

Classical scholars have long recognized that Greek and Latin literature relies extensively on the technique called ring composition. The technique is already fully developed in the poetry of Homer; indeed, the entire *Iliad* may be read as a vast ring composition of almost unbelievable complexity and sophistication. Its irreducible quantum is repetition of individual words, phrases, and motifs or themes. At its most elementary level, ring composition involves the statement of a given word at or near the beginning of a poem, work, or section thereof, and the repetition of this word at or near the end. It is proper to speak of ring composition even if the words are not exactly identical, for synonyms will discharge the same function of tying beginning to end. Nor need the repeated elements be restricted to an individual word, but may involve phrases of either identical or synonymous vocabulary. Finally, such phrases combine into motifs and themes, and from these cumulative verbal amalgams follows the development of the larger ring structures of themes that organize the larger work.

But its purely formal and organizational role is usually not the sole or even major reason for the existence of the ring. Its role is much more closely related to the meaning of the work than to its organization, more to its ideas than to its structure—even though both ends are achieved.

Thematically, the *Iliad* ends as it began: a father comes to claim a child from an enemy and offers handsome recompense as ransom. At the opening of the *Iliad*, the priest Chryses comes to Agamemnon to ransom back his daughter Chryseis; the priest is unsuccessful, and as a result a plague descends on the Greek camp. At the end of the poem, some 15,000 lines later, a father, Priam, king of Troy, comes to ransom his son, the slain Hector, from Achilles; the king is successful, and the poem comes to a conclusion on this strong note of reconciliation and the muting of grand and savage passions. The two ransom scenes stand as frames around the entire poem. The format of the scenes (A wants B from C, and C will/will not give B to A) is reiterated perhaps scores of times throughout the length of the poem in relationships on both the human and the divine level, not the least of which is that of the eternal triangle (two men want one woman, two women want one man). At the end, the theme is seen against the backdrop of the many times it has been introduced in the course of the poem and not been worked out satisfactorily. This frame provides a kind of structural integrity to the epic, but, more importantly, by its initial and concluding positions in the work, it calls attention to the significance of that theme of which it is a particular manifestation in each instance.

Such frames do not stand only at the extremes of a poem (or novel). A multiplicity of internal rings also organizes the smaller modules of the larger whole, and these smaller rings may or may not be related to the larger ones in theme and language.

Greek prose writers constantly use ring composition to organize the structure of their works and, simultaneously, to comment on the themes. The Latin writers, knowing their Greek well and understanding quite thoroughly how Greek literature was put together, adopted this device of ring composition in their own works. At the end of Book 8 of the *Aeneid*, for example, the goddess Venus returns to her son Aeneas with splendid weapons and a shield which the divine smith Vulcan has forged for him. This shield is a marvel to behold, for on it are represented the past (relative to Aeneas) history of Rome as well as the future, stretching down to Vergil's own day. On a very basic level, the long description of the shield (beginning at line 626 with *Illic* . . . , "There . . . "), consisting of over one hundred lines (626–728), is framed by the repeated and synonymous vocabulary at start and conclusion.

A 617 rejoicing at honor
B 619 marvels at
C 625 the shield
D 626 There . . .
C 729 throughout the shield
B 730 does he marvel
A 730 in pictures he delights

In the framing sections, the Latin vocabulary is arranged in an extended chiastic form, as is suggested above by the somewhat forced English word order (note especially the As and Bs). The meter itself underscores the ring composition in that equivalent metrical positions are employed for several of the key terms and phrases. At the conclusion of the description of the shield, the return to the language that prefaces it creates a ring composition that is a graphic depiction not only of the circular "ring" of the physical shield, but also of the psychological unity or wholeness emblematic of the task Aeneas now quite literally lifts up.

Similar instances of ring composition are to be found in Burroughs, as for example at 5.104. Tarzan and two apes, disguised as Arabs, have attacked a village in order to rescue Jane. Taglat, one of the apes, is filled with fanciful notions of his own about Jane, and he absconds with the woman. Tarzan sets out in pursuit, and the near-rescue is framed, like the little jungle enclave where the ape has taken the woman, by two references to the glade itself.

Tarzan, roaming the jungle in search of the trail of Taglat and the she, traveled swiftly. *In a* little moonlit *glade* ahead of him the great ape was bending over the prostrate form of the woman Tarzan sought.

Tarzan passed within fifty yards of the tragedy that was being enacted *in the glade,* and the opportunity was gone beyond recall.

The scene is framed, and is therefore made to stand out in all its teasing eroticism, by the traveling of Tarzan and by the reference to the glade itself and the little drama ("tragedy") in it. The brief digression that describes what Taglat is trying to do is therefore joined smoothly to the larger narrative by the epic device of ring composition which here takes the form of both a motif (traveling search of Tarzan) and a word ("glade").

Let us consider another example. Tarzan has just discovered that Mbonga the witch doctor, whom he had thought of as a god, is in reality nothing but a shrivelled old man. Mbonga tries to kill him and Tarzan is about to plunge his knife into the scrawny neck of the witch doctor, when "something stayed the ape-man's hand." Tarzan leaves. But he is puzzled by the episode, and when he retires to his sleeping place for the night, he ponders the matter: "It was late when Tarzan sought a *swaying couch* among the trees beneath which slept the apes of Kerchak, and *he was still absorbed in the solution of his strange problem* when he fell asleep" (6.59). After he wakens the next morning, he sees an orchid and begins to wonder about its origins, its ways and its purposes, and even about himself. Tarzan is trying to define the concept of God in his mind. His reasoning is interrupted, however, by the wailing scream of a baby ape who has been caught in the coils of a snake. *"Tarzan almost had arrived at something tangible* when a distant wail startled him from his preoccupation into sensibility of the present and the real. The wail came from the jungle at some distance from Tarzan's *swaying couch"* (6.60). The repetition of the phrase "swaying couch" and the allusion to solving a problem at the beginning and the end of this "intellectual" interlude in the action-filled sequence of young Tarzan's life in the jungle clearly demarcates the passage in the typical epic fashion. It is also clear that the informing polarity of deed-word or action-thought underpins the larger narrative sequence. The action is filled with movement:

Tarzan . . . swung himself into the branches of the tree . . . [6.59].

Tarzan was electrified into instant action. Like an arrow from a bow he shot through the trees in the direction of the sound [6.60].

Sandwiched between these two framing references to action arising from arduous physical activity is the serene and restful passage which establishes Tarzan's dawning awareness of the nonphysical, spiritual aspects of existence. That passage is itself framed by the phrase "swaying couch."

Schematically, the section (6.59-60) looks as follows:

> A ACTION
>   B THOUGHT ("couch-problem")
>   B THOUGHT ("solution-couch")
> A ACTION

A chiastic frame, which by definition consists of four parts and by its very nature is more forceful than a two-part frame, concentrates interest on the enclosed sequence and emphasizes its importance.

A series of unifying rings imposes a structural coherence on *Tales;* thematic elements introduced at the beginning of the work appear towards the end and in this way bring the reader full circle. In the first example, from Chapter 2, Tarzan is watching the warriors of Mbonga's village dig a pit for trapping animals (6.24). In the second, from Chapter 11, he also observes the natives attempting to set a trap for a lion (6.162). The two passages recall each other (cf. especially ". . . having watched them at it upon other occasions" at 6.162), not only in the similarity of the theme of traps and baiting, but also in the larger context of ring composition.

In the opening passage, the pit the warriors make is designed to capture a huge animal such as the elephant. Tarzan does realize at last what the point of the pit is, and, knowing that his friend Tantor the elephant is moving in the direction of the pit, he races with deliberate speed to warn the animal. In the nick of time he arrives at the edge of the concealed trap and warns off the elephant, but, trying to leave before the hunters arrive, Tarzan falls into the pit. It is Tarzan, not Tantor, who has been trapped, and the natives carry him back to their village. Before they can kill him, however, Tantor comes to the rescue, and as the elephant was saved by Tarzan, so he in turn saves Tarzan. This chapter is thus self-contained and is itself constructed on the general principle of "end-returning-to-beginning." The rescuer is rescued.

But what interests us in the overall structure of the book is not so much the free-standing unity of the second chapter of the book, but its clear relationship to the latter part of *Tales*, Chapter 11 ("A Jungle Joke"), for here the antithesis of Chapter 2 is set out. To recapitulate, Chapter 2 deals with Tarzan's rescue of Tantor from a trap which the hunters have built, his capture by them as a consequence of his rescuing of the elephant, and the elephant's reciprocal rescue of Tarzan. Chapter 11 sets forth Tarzan's eventual rescue of a lion who was caught in the trap and the trapping of one of the natives, as if in balance to his own entrapment in Chapter 2. This sense of reciprocity in trapping and being trapped is also brought out within this one chapter (11). Through a pun, Burroughs underscores the balance of the relationship, for the natives were "placing and baiting a trap for Numa, the lion" (6.162), and, in turn, "the baiting of the blacks was Tarzan's chief divertisment" (6.162).

Here, then, the trapped has become the trapper, and one of the trappers has become the trapped. The symmetrical reversal is epic in conception, and the more elaborate execution in Chapter 11 derives from the eight chapters that intervene between 2 and 11. For a number of themes investigated in those central chapters are reintroduced in Chapter 11 for further elaboration (for example, Tarzan's disguise by means of an animal skin, and exposure of a witch doctor to be killed by animals).

The relationship between Chapter 2 and Chapter 11 is first indicated by the thematic ring composition in the "trapping" passages alluded to above. But Burroughs' technique is so like the epic that, with Homeric fullness, this relationship is brought to our unavoidable attention through additional cases of ring composition.

When Tarzan is brought into their compound as a captive, he is set upon and taunted by the villagers (6.33f.), and similar treatment befalls Numa the lion when he is brought into the village (6.169f.). Further, in Chapter 2, Tarzan's control over Tantor is accounted for as follows: "It was the power of the man-mind over that of the brute . . . " (6.27). The point is repeated in Chapter 11 in connection with Tarzan's reputation as a result of his grizzly trickery on Mbonga's people: "in the mysterious haunts of the savage jungle where he ranged, mightiest of beasts because of the man-mind which directed his giant muscles and his flawless courage" (6.174).

Chapter 2 gives a graphic description of the incredible damage Tantor does in the village (6.36); Chapter 11 presents a similar account of the carnage the freed lion wreaks among the villagers (6.174). In short, there can be no serious question of the intentional correspondence between the two chapters, the point of which, as we saw, was the working out of a symmetrical reversal in which hunted and hunter exchange roles. Finally, it can be noted that Chapter 2 is the second chapter of the book, and Chapter 11 the second to the last chapter of the book.

Tales has more ring composition of this thematic type, and it is related to the trapping and rescuing we have discussed for Chapters 2 and 11. Similar connections are made between Chapters 1 and 12, the first and last chapters of the book.

In Chapter 1, Tarzan learns beyond question that his nature is fundamentally different from that of the apes with whom he has grown up and still lives. He has not yet fully defined what these differences are, and the whole book is in large part concerned with this basic problem of self-definition. (This theme is as old as Homer, and Burroughs has already worked with it in *Jewels*.) By the end of the book Tarzan comes full circle in this quest for a personal identity, for the apes "knew he was different. Tarzan knew it too; but he was glad that he was—he was a MAN" (6.187).

In Chapter 1, the hunters of Mbonga's tribe have built a cage on a jungle trail and concealed it (6.17). Tarzan's first rival in love, the ape Taug, has wandered into the trap set by the hunters and has been carried off to their village. Without fully knowing why he does it, Tarzan comes to the rescue of his fierce rival and frees him from the prison devised by Mbonga's hunters (6.22).

In the final chapter of the book, Taug recollects this scene along with many other scenes that have taken place between Chapters 1 and 12. The ape considers the totality of his relationship with Tarzan and finally takes a stand in favor of Tarzan, the outsider, against the attacks proposed by the other apes of the tribe. Here, as in the nexus between Chapters 2 and 11, the connection between Chapters 1 and 12 is based on a symmetrical reversal. Tarzan, who initially did not know what or who he was (6.21), and Taug were fiercest enemies but in the conclusion Tarzan has discovered, and is proud of the fact (6.187), that he is a man, and Taug has become his friend and mighty ally. Ring composition, as well as the interweaving recapitulation of themes explored throughout the book, is again the formal technique that brings out the thematic development and portrayal of personal growth.

This thematic ring composition has more than a casual affinity with that which frames the *Iliad*, in which a symmetrical reversal also takes place. At the conclusion of the *Iliad*, the Greek leader Achilles has conquered his wrath and has ransomed back a child to its father, but in the opening of the poem the Greek leader Agamemnon, overcome with wrath, refuses to give back a child to its father. Growth and maturation of human identity are among the most basic themes in Greek and Latin literature, and Burroughs, by employing the technique of ring composition to delineate the relationship between Chapters 1 and 12, places these themes prominently before us in *Tales*. Finally, just as Chapters 1 and 12 deal with Tarzan's relationship to the world of his "people," the apes—with his "socialization" —so Chapters 2 and 11 examine his relationship both to the people of Mbonga's village and to the animals of the jungle. The chapters themselves, then, as modular units in the overall organization of the novel, fall into an emerging chiastic structure.

A   Chapter 1 (Tarzan and apes)
  B   Chapter 2 (Tarzan, natives, animals
              other than apes)
  B   Chapter 11 (Tarzan, natives, animals
              other than apes)
A   Chapter 12 (Tarzan and apes)

This point need not come as a surprise to us, for it merely shows at the thematic level the identical dynamics of organization that lie at the root of individual phrases or sentences of the sort we analyzed earlier. Nor should we be surprised that Chapters 3 and 10 of *Tales* display a continuation of this balanced composition. The intervening chapters are themselves arranged in the structure of ring composition and lend to the novel the unmistakable imprint of

Homeric epic. It may be added that central to the novel's ring composition is the episode that deals with the theme of fraudulence in organized religion and relates to Burroughs' controlling vision in this novel of Tarzan's discovery of a principle in the universe that is mightier than himself. For like the style of sentences, this technique is inextricably and totally intertwined with meaning.

Ring composition and the occasionally indistinguishable technique of parallelism form—at least in *Tales*—the structural backbone to which the thematic core and, ultimately, the sense of the narrative are attached. Remove this essential structure, and the emerging sense of Tarzan's identity and beliefs collapse into a jumbled heap of *passim* observations. Only the true painter may be aware of the skeletal structure that exists beneath the lifelike figure, but no one fails to recognize a clumsy amateur's figure-painting, conceived as it is in muddled confusion and an imperfect understanding of underlying anatomy.

At the start of *Jewels*, Tarzan has set out on an expedition to Opar for more gold to cover losses he has suffered in a fraudulent venture. The theme of the loss of identity, first indicated at 5.36 after Tarzan's awakening from unconsciousness, is balanced by its opposite, the recovery of identity (5.143). As frames for the central "elaboration" of some 110 pages, the two passages obviously constitute a ring composition.

Before the opening element of this ring and after its concluding element stands another ring composition which deals with Werper, the Belgian villain in the book. He has murdered his superior officer and is in flight (5.8), but at 5.144 the authorities catch up with him. Again, the two passages are clearly related, and they provide the partial framing structure for the book.

The references to the supposed death of Mugambi provides another framing role. Mugambi had been left in charge of Tarzan's estate when Tarzan set out for Opar, and it was Mugambi who supervised the hopeless defense of the bungalow when it was attacked by the raiding Arabs under Achmet Zek. The buildings are put to the torch (5.35). Mugambi, once believed dead, returns alive at the end: "It was Mugambi, whom Jane had thought dead amidst the charred ruins of the bungalow. Ah, such a reunion!" (5.157). The thematic point of this ring composition is to present a variation of the book's underlying theme of death and resurrection as it is manifested in the "death" of Tarzan (cf. the sepulchral imagery of the description of his "death" at 5.36) and his subsequent rebirth.

Return is not without its important use of ring composition. Tarzan and the Waziri make a trip to fabled Opar in order to bring back gold (2.160–211). After he has been captured and almost sacrificed by the Oparians, Tarzan is ensconced by the high priestess, La, in a dark room apparently unknown to any other Oparian. Burroughs describes the winding passages, hidden shafts, and "tantalizing apertures" (cf. 2.207) through which Tarzan moves before finally stumbling on the route by which to extricate himself from Opar. He has discovered a secret passageway from and to Opar.

Fifty Oparians, hunting for Tarzan, come upon Jane by Tarzan's cabin, and they abduct her to become a sacrifice on the altar of La. Tarzan, upon learning from his apes that a "white she" has been carried off by the gnarled men of Opar, rushes to the rescue. When he approaches Opar, he retraces, in reverse and abbreviated order, his previous trip out in order to get back in once more. His knowledge of the secret passage is essential to his reaching the woman being sacrificed before it is too late. The description of Tarzan's penetration of Opar for a second time (2.206) clearly recalls the earlier passage at 2.185ff. The first entry into Opar had been for the express purpose of finding the gold treasure of which Tarzan had learned from the Waziri (2.128, 160), but the second visit to Opar is for a different kind of treasure. The two passages are tied together on the obvious level of the ring composition, but it becomes more than a structural link in that it calls attention to the differing motivations that impel Tarzan to the City of Gold. And in that more important role the ring composition proves to be a means for evaluating or assessing a protagonist who, rather than a cardboard figure of unidimensional proportions, is a complex character whose emotional and appetitive life is quite unpredictable. In brief, there is more to Tarzan than greed, although, being human and having lived in a modern civilization, he is not without this all too human characteristic (2.128).

The ring composition, then, unites the entire sequence of the extended narrative of Opar, which may be summarized in the following way: Tarzan and fifty Waziri set out for Opar to take treasure; Tarzan escapes through winding underground passages. Fifty

Oparians set out for the jungle to recapture Tarzan, but take Jane
instead; Tarzan returns to Opar by the same underground passages.
If we take into consideration the central episodes within Opar, the
attempted sacrifices of both Tarzan (2.169) and Jane (2.208), the
skeleton or frame of the Opar account (2.160–211) may be presented
as indicated in the following outline.

> A   Tarzan and Waziri go to Opar, get gold.
>   B   Tarzan is almost sacrificed.
>   C   La is almost killed.
>   B   Tarzan escapes from Opar.
> A   Tarzan and Waziri return with gold.
>
> A'   Oparians go to jungle fort, get Jane.
>   B'   Tarzan returns to Opar.
>   C'   Jane is almost sacrificed.
>   B'   Tarzan escapes from Opar with Jane.
> A'   Oparians pursue couple, but give up.

A basic symmetry in the underlying organization of the Opar
narrative does emerge from this analysis, and it is the kind of classical balance of episodes that ring composition promotes so successfully in Homeric poetry. This balance is, of course, merely an
extension of the implications of the style of individual sentences.

The full complexity of this structure has not been completely
unraveled, for interwoven with the Opar account is the larger
balancing moment of the Tennington expedition with all of its little
rivalries and jealousies. Indeed, the theme of jealousy is the thread that
knits together the Opar and Tennington stories. These triangular relationships of erotic jealousy are numerous: Tennington, Thuran (alias Rokoff),
Hazel Strong (2.111, 203f.); Clayton, Thuran, Jane (2.177); Tarzan, Tha,
La (2.171); Tarzan, Jane, Clayton (2.101. 183, 191, 213); and Tarzan, Jane,
Olga de Coude (2.214). This last triangle quite clearly recalls the roles of
the de Coudes at the novel's opening, in which an unhappy and
potentially ruinous triangular relationship develops among Count
de Coude, his wife Olga, and Tarzan. Through the device of ring
composition and the parallel development of an important theme,
erotic jealousy, a tightly knit unity is imposed upon the book. Its
many seemingly discrete narratives are gathered together into one.

The possibility for violent eruptions from these jealousies is quashed at the end of the novel with its double wedding—an age-old device for symbolizing the unification and harmonizing of personal and social disruptions. The wedding of Tarzan and Jane at the end of *Return* is connected to the wedding of Lord and Lady Greystoke, Tarzan's parents, at the beginning of *Tarzan* (1.2); the two weddings are related by the thematic ring composition.

Finally, let us consider some examples of ring composition in *Tarzan*. The first two chapters of the book deal with Tarzan's real parents and the mutinous crew that put them ashore on the African coast. In the last chapter of the book, indeed in its very last sentence, Tarzan addresses himself to the fact that he "never knew who my father was" (2.245). The antithesis of the crew that took over the *Fuwalda* is the crew of Frenchmen that discovers the Porter party on the same beach on which the Greystokes had been set ashore some twenty years earlier (1.157ff.); where the *Fuwalda*'s men were all but animals in their behavior, the Frenchmen are courteous, brave, and sympathetic. The connection between these two crews is mediated by the incident in which the Porter group is set ashore by a crew that also has mutinied (1.134, 145, 160), and all three sets are related to the boat which Tarzan and D'Arnot charter to return for Professor Porter's treasure. It will be recalled that Tarzan's parents had chartered a boat, the *Fuwalda*, to reach their destination.

A month later they arrived at Freetown, where they chartered a small sailing vessel, the *Fuwalda*, which was to bear them to their destination. [1.3]

Shortly after the episode of the lion hunt, D'Arnot succeeded in chartering an ancient tub for the coastwise trip to Tarzan's land-locked harbor. [1.220]

Both of these ships arrive at the same beach, the latter by design and the former by force. The ships form a kind of structural frame tying together separate destinies that come to overlap.

   A   Charter of *Fuwalda* to get to Africa: mutiny, death
      B   Charter of *Arrow*: mutiny, death, exposure
         C   Spanish galleon: mutiny, death, rescue
      B   French cruiser: death, rescue
   A   Charter of tub to get Porter's treasure: return

The central episode, narrated by Jane Porter in a letter to her friend Hazel Strong, explains the reason for the Porters' journey to Africa. In view of the close similarity between the mutinous events on the Spanish galleon some time in the late 1540s and those on the *Fuwalda* and the *Arrow*, it is perhaps debatable whether we should be speaking of ring composition or thematic parallelism. The net result is to bring the reader back to the opening complications of the novel and to depict a certain parallel working out of human destinies.

The iterativeness of human existence is, as the repetitions in his style and themes suggest, of no small interest to Burroughs. This is not to say that all events and all lives are exactly parallel, but only that the starting point for the development of individual variations is often emphasized. Burroughs invites the reader to draw certain inferences about the role of treasure, or money, in the civilized world to which Tarzan is violently introduced when white men arrive in his jungle. These boats and their mutinies provide the occasion for commentary on the corrupting and destructive role of money—as Jane says in her letter to Hazel (1.145).

There is, then, perhaps a certain irony in the fact that the Greystokes, who suffered more than all the groups that appear in the theme, set out for Africa with ostensibly nonmaterial motives. They supposedly came not to seek treasure, but to investigate the mistreatment of black English subjects (1.2). But Lord Greystoke was impelled not by purely humanitarian motives, but by "political ambition" and his understanding that the "delicate and important commission" was "a stepping stone to posts of greater importance and responsibility" (1.2). Like the other characters examined through the theme, Greystoke, too, had very human, if less directly material, reasons for undertaking an arduous journey. Thus ring composition and parallelism connect the passages to each other, thereby providing a commentary on the contrasts between civilization and jungle.

Polarity is not, strictly speaking, a technique, but like the ancient writers, Burroughs developed it beyond a mere convenience of language. Consider, for example, the polarity at 2.159, where the extremes of physical decrepitude and vigor are artfully presented. Chapter 18 concludes with a dark account of human behavior after extremes of physical privation and debility; Chapter 19 opens brightly with a description of Tarzan's "great, rolling muscles, the personification of physical perfection and strength." The polar depiction involving the "civilized" Clayton and Thuran, on the one hand, and the "savage" Tarzan, on the other, accentuates the physical state of each and brings out with forceful irony what is perhaps Burroughs' most abiding polarity, that of civilization-jungle.

The French anthropologist Claude Lévi-Strauss has made fashionable the polarity raw-cooked, as in the title of volume one of his *Introduction to a Science of Mythology*.[1] In synoptic terms, raw and cooked stand, respectively, for savagery and civilization, barbarism and culture, jungle and civilization. The polarity is known from Greek culture in somewhat the same sense, as when the savage and uncivilized cyclops, Polyphemus, eats Odysseus' men raw, while the civilized Greeks always cook their meat (leaving aside for the moment the barbarous practice of the cyclops' cannibalism). Burroughs, too, uses this important polarity at 3.43: "'Mugambi built a fire and *cooked* his portion of the kill; but Tarzan, Sheeta, and Akut tore theirs, *raw*, with their sharp teeth, growling among themselves when one ventured to encroach upon the share of another." [Italics added] The polarity is especially pointed here, for it reverses the traditional connotations. The eaters of raw meat are ultimately the most "civilized" in this book, with its almost macabre fascination for cannibalism and eating. Food and eating become a means for expressing the deep-seated polarity of jungle-civilization. The inversion that construes the raw as the uncivilized, but less desirable because hypocritical, is brought out even more forcefully at 5.15.

And so Tarzan always came back to Nature in the spirit of a lover keeping a long deferred tryst after a period behind prison walls. His Waziri, at marrow, were more civilized than he. They cooked their meat before they ate it and they shunned many articles of food as unclean that Tarzan had eaten with gusto all his life and so insidious is the virus of hypocrisy that even the stalwart ape-man hesitated to give rein to his natural longings before them. He ate burnt flesh when he would have preferred it raw and unspoiled.

In the moral judgment which Burroughs passes on the world of Tarzan and the larger world of civilized, especially European, society, it is clear that civilization, for all its wonders and achievements, comes off second best to the jungle.

Time also provides a convenient source of polarity in literature. The past affects the future, for good and bad, and ancient literature recognized the fact. The most striking example is perhaps the relationship between the temporal polarities, which is explored in Aeschylus' great trilogy, the *Oresteia*. The examination of the extremes of time is as important to an understanding of that trilogy as it is for an awareness of Burroughs' manipulation of the temporal nexus in which Tarzan is constantly seen as a participant. The polarity is perhaps most often manifested as the contrast between the time or circumstances of the life of Tarzan's father and of Tarzan himself. Tied to the full development of the polarity are certain symbolic items such as the knife that had belonged to Tarzan's father, the cabin built by his father, and even the genetic heritage of Tarzan from his father and earlier ancestors.

Some polarities form the basis for thematic expansion, others do not; some are readily documented in ancient writers, others are not. Implicit in all, however, is the notion of the deeper examination or the more elaborate analysis of a person or situation which the double viewpoint affords. For example, if a writer wants to talk about the concept "mankind," he can refer to it in a variety of ways and influence his audience's perception of the concept accordingly. The following are possible polar expressions for mankind: men and women, free men and slaves, Greeks and barbarians, children and adults, soldiers and farmers, thinkers and doers. It is clear that the specific formulation employed predisposes a reader or listener to understand the concept in a highly specific way, and thus the author is able to focus with unobtrusive precision on the particular point of view he wants the audience to adopt about mankind. Thus, a polarity such as Greek-barbarian (or Roman-barbarian) becomes a means in ancient literature for talking about the nature of civilization (as in Herodotus or Caesar); and in Burroughs the simple polarity of raw-cooked with reference to food eaten by characters becomes a springboard for talking about the reality and the appearance of civilized behavior.

The following list of polarities in Burroughs is representative, but not exhaustive: violence-gentleness (2.45), man-beast (2.80), noise-silence (2.69, 3.32), war-peace (5.117), havoc-peace (5.48), happiness-heartbreak (5.72), life-death (5.120), and friend-enemy (5.122).

Related to the idea of polarity, if not to the precise expression of it, is that of juxtaposition, of which polarity is, after all, a special case. Some instances of juxtaposition are the panther-like violence of Tarzan set against the dainty heedlessness of the deer (3.28); the trussed tutor abandoning his hysteria in favor of the use of reason (4.18); Werper fleeing the Arab village while Mugambi sneaks into it (5.56); jungle life divided into the hunters and the hunted (5.78); thoughts of marriage amid imminent death (2.158); Jane working her way through "a thorny boma wall with her delicate hands" (3.102); on a quiet and peaceful voyage a ship suddenly blowing up with great destructive force (3.139); Korak moving with grace while the ape Akut waddles along "in marked contrast to the awkwardness of his companion" (4.65); Meriem escaping a lion and Baynes looking for one (4.134f.); as a lion attacks, Baynes falling apart, while Meriem and Korak remain cool in the face of danger (4.150f.). In all of these cases, as well as many others scattered throughout the corpus, the sum of the total contrast, both the strictly verbal and the thematic, is greater than the juxtaposed parts individually.

Polarity, juxtaposition, contrast—all are essentially similar modes in conception, though somewhat different in the verbal or thematic execution. In ancient literature, especially the biographical tradition, it was not uncommon for a writer to set up explicit parallels that both compared similarities and contrasted differences among various individuals or situations. The formal designation for this device is synkrisis, or, quite simply, comparison. It is a favorite technique in Burroughs.[2]

Synkrisis is direct comparison, for the explicit purposes of contrastive judgment, of individual animals, humans, or events. The comparison is direct, but is neither formally stated through *like* or *as* as in the simile, nor implied by the figurative language as in the metaphor. Rather, the comparison is inferential and, in effect, unavoidable. At the simplest level of organization, synkrisis compares a specific person with another person in a specific context. Through repeated use, however, a more general and encompassing system of comparison is developed, so that one may speak about large sections of formally parallel but ideationally contrasting units of discourse—the parallel plot.

In the Homeric *Odyssey*, for example, a running synkrisis is developed around the notion of actual marriage and connubial relationships. Comparison is drawn among the situations of Penelope and the suitors, Penelope and Odysseus, Odysseus and Calypso, Odysseus and Circe, Arete and Alcinous, Odysseus and Nausicaa, Hephaistos and Aphrodite, Ares and Aphrodite, Laertes and Anticleia, Menelaus and Helen, Agamemnon and Clytemnestra, to name a few. The evaluative comparisons are not intended to be matched up one for one but function like echoing reverberations throughout the work. That is to say, for instance, that our final assessment of the marriage of Odysseus and Penelope as a cohesive and healing force within a rent society emerges not only from the internal evidence of that one relationship, but also from the direct comparison of, for example, that of Arete and Alcinous (unifying) or of Odysseus and Circe (destructive). Only when seen as one of many or even countless possible marriage arrangements can the given one of Penelope and Odysseus be intelligently assessed.

The particular manifestation of the synkristic form in terms of father and son is rather common. Greek comedy, both the older type associated with the name of Aristophanes and the newer type associated with Menander and the early Roman comedians, places strong reliance on this fundamental synkrisis that barely masks a sustained battle of the generations.

To begin with one of the more specific synkrises encountered in Burroughs, we may direct attention to the type which juxtaposes Tarzan to his uncle or cousin, the putative heir and heir-apparent to the distinguished title of Lord Greystoke. Here the apeman is seen in the jungle environment and is engaged in some "barbarous" activity; the others are in their urban surroundings and are busied in some "civilized" social diversion. A typical passage is an early one in *Tarzan* (1.69f.). Tarzan has been pursuing the native who shot his stepmother and for the first time has seen a human being eat food that has been cooked by fire. After the man leaves the part of the slain boar that he does not eat, Tarzan partakes of the remnants.

But, be that as it may, Tarzan would not ruin good meat in any such foolish manner, so he gobbled down a great quantity of the raw flesh, burying the balance of the carcass beside the trail where he could find it upon his return.

And then Lord Greystoke wiped his greasy fingers upon his naked thighs and took up the trail of Kulonga, the son of Mbonga, the king; while in far-off London another Lord Greystoke, the younger brother of the real Lord Greystoke's father, sent back his chops to the club's *chef* because they were underdone, and when he had finished his repast he dropped his finger-ends into a silver bowl of scented water and dried them upon a piece of snowy damask.

The antitheses leap out from the page. The phrase "gobbled down a great quantity of the raw flesh" is opposed to "sent back his chops to the club's *chef* because they were underdone," and "wiped his greasy fingers upon his naked thighs" to "dropped his finger-ends into a silver bowl of scented water and dried them upon a piece of snowy damask." The underlying polarity of the "raw and the cooked," the uncivilized and the civilized, is quite unmistakable. Equally unmistakable is the contrast between the crisp and unfussy vigor of Tarzan's behavior and the wearied effeteness of the uncle's comportment in far-off London. The passage, based on a polarity of archetypal antiquity for describing the inherent antagonism between barbarity and culture, reinterprets the connotations of the traditional categories in such a way that the raw, the uncivilized, has emerged as the more desirable pole of the antithesis. At the same time that the savage ways of the jungle are extolled, those of London and the larger world of civilization are implicitly decried. The inner logic of the praise-blame polarity makes the contrast inevitable. Synkrisis, it will be seen, can offer the author a very powerful rhetorical technique for laying out and directing attention to the underlying attitudes that obtain in his world.

Quite indicative of the judgmental use of synkrisis for purposes of auctorial biasing is the passage in which Burroughs describes the loss of La's sacrificial knife from the religious rites in the forgotten kingdom of Opar.

The sacred knife was gone! Handed down through countless ages it had come to her as a heritage and an insignia of her religious office and regal authority from some long-dead progenitor of lost and forgotten Atlantis. The loss of the crown jewels of the Great Seal of England could have brought no greater consternation to a British king than did the pilfering of the sacred knife bring to La, the Oparian, Queen and High Priestess of the degraded remnants of the oldest civilization upon earth [5.64].

By drawing these comparisons between the British realm and the kingdom of Opar, Burroughs implicitly comments on the attitudes he wishes the reader to adopt concerning the Oparians. They are to be taken seriously and, as the subsequent "history" of the civilization makes clear, their kingdom is not to be considered insignificant. In such indirect fashion, the author elevates the significance of the environment in which his protagonist acts; and if the hero is involved with the numinous foundations of a civilization, the hero must in himself be of some significance. The comparison, though ostensibly made between Opar and England, is in reality designed to enhance the importance of Tarzan and the symbolic knife. The search for the knife will run parallel to the search for the missing jewels and for Tarzan's own personality; each in its way has a fundamental importance, a point brought out by the initial synkrisis.

There are literally hundreds of examples of synkrisis in Burroughs, and some more prevalent types may be noted. Tarzan versus his uncle (as in the example cited above), Tarzan versus other men, primitive versus advanced societies, animals versus men, Tarzan versus the reader, the world of nature versus the world of human artifacts, jungle versus city, Tarzan's real mother (Lady Alice) versus his foster mother (Kala), and Tarzan versus his son are just a few.

Although synkrisis constitutes one of the most important modes of comparison in Burroughs works and permits a reasonably consistent view of major themes and characters to emerge, it is by no means the only comparative form with solid classical antecedents. If synkrisis is direct comparison, for the purpose of contrastive judgment, of individual characters or events, simile is the explicit and metaphor the implicit comparison of single words, characters, concepts, or events for very similar ends.

Among the most common types of similes in Burroughs' corpus are those drawn from the world of animals. If one looks back to the epic models of both Homer and Vergil, it becomes clear that the comparison of man in his many capacities to the nonhuman creatures of the animal kingdom enjoys a respectable antiquity. Even by the time Homer's poems were fixed, a fairly well-established set of equivalences seems to have been adopted. Certain animals are thought of as timid, others as courageous, still others as cunning, and so forth. The fondness for the animal fable in earlier Greek poetry attests to this reliance on the traditionally accepted qualities of an animal to suggest or connote certain human characteristics. Homeric lions, for example, have a tendency to be depicted as strong (*Iliad* 5.299, 12.42, 16.826) and aggressive attackers (*Iliad* 5.161, 10.485, 15.630); doves are generally timorous (*Iliad* 22.140, 23.874), as are hares and lambs (*Iliad* 22.310). Therefore, when an individual is compared to an animal such as a lion, a certain preconceived and traditionally sanctioned connotation is associated with him. Burroughs not only draws on this earlier tradition which is ready-made for him but also develops to some extent a certain internally consistent set of valuations.

When Tarzan suspects he is being attacked in the darkness of the night by a stealthy prowler, he says "Who is it. . . that creeps upon Tarzan of the Apes, like a hungry lion out of the darkness?" (3.87) As we have seen, the lion is established in the epic tradition as an aggressive attacker, and it is to this model that Tarzan is made to appeal. So much greater the surprise when the intruder turns out to be the old hag Tambudza, who has come to help rather than harm Tarzan.

The lion's courage is also to be noted in Burroughs, as in the dramatic scene in which Alice Clayton, Tarzan's real mother, saves her husband's life. "She had always been afraid of firearms, and would never touch them, but now she rushed toward the ape with the fearlessness of a lioness protecting its young." (1.23) This particular passage is, incidentally, very like a Homeric prototype. At *Iliad* 17.132ff. a fierce battle is raging over the body of the slain Patroklos. The Trojans wish to recover the body for mutilation, but the Greeks resist this effront in every possible way.

> But Ajax planted himself, covering over the son of Menoiteus (viz. Patroklos) with his broad shield, as a lion covers his offspring if hunters meet him in the forest as he is carrying his young; and the lion rejoices in his strength, hiding his eyes as he furrows his entire brow; in this way did Ajax take his stand about the hero Patroklos.

Though not as full as the Homeric example, Burroughs' comparison is part of a lengthy tradition which sees in the lion a paradigm of the exemplary courage of a parent protecting its offspring. Neither Ajax in Homer nor Alice in Burroughs, it should be observed, is in fact protecting offspring.

The opposite pole of the comparison of human courage to that of an animal is the likening of human timidity to that of a deer or gazelle. Similes that make use of these animals, especially the former, are not at all uncommon in the Homeric corpus (for example, *Iliad* 1.225ff., 11.113–121).

At a point in *Tarzan*, Jane Porter thinks she may have been abandoned by her new protector in the jungle. When he suddenly reappears with food and comfort for her tense nerves, she develops a typical reaction. "She did not lose consciousness, but she clung tightly to him, shuddering and trembling like a frightened deer" (1.165). This simile sets the tone for most of the subsequent ones which employ the deer, fear, and trembling. To it is added the notion of cowardice, as in some of the Homeric examples. In an interesting section in *Tales*, Tarzan has discovered what it means to dream and is very puzzled by what he considers an abnormality. He does not stay to fight those monsters and great beasts who populate his dreams. Instead he uncharacteristically turns to flight.

> Then he commenced to wonder if some of these strange creatures which he met in his sleep might not slay him, for at such times Tarzan of the Apes seemed to be a different Tarzan, sluggish, helpless, timid—wishing to flee his enemies as fled Bara, the deer, most fearful of creatures[6.137].

Just as Homer makes implicit judgments about the individuals whom he is comparing to the animals, so Burroughs steps into his work and orients the reader to his own attitudes. There are many other animal similes in Burroughs, some of which have obvious analogues in Homer (for example, sheep, dogs, and wolves), and it will be sufficient to list some of them in a footnote for the reader's private consideration.[3]

In Homer, simile is perhaps a more vivid device for the author's entry into the poem's world than metaphor, but metaphor is in general an active trope in Greek and Latin literature. One of the more consistent metaphorical systems in Burroughs involves the conception of the jungle as an animate creature, at times one with "hungers." If one can speak of metaphors based on orality, one could certainly find an author less productive of such metaphors. In fact, like the Homer of the *Odyssey*, Burroughs does have a sharply etched fascination for language and thematic developments that center on eating and ingestion, the most obvious manifestations of which are the numerous passages in which Tarzan kills and eats his prey with graphic gusto. The hunger of the jungle is most clearly brought out in those phrases in which it "swallows" someone (for example, 4.35 and 5.188). Such a metaphorical usage is not original with Burroughs, but the sustained appeal to these "oral" metaphors drawn from the description of animal functions and anatomy makes it necessary to think of the jungle as itself alive. Many of these metaphorical uses are not striking or arresting in their novelty, but through constant repetition they do demonstrate his understanding of the jungle.

A paragraph near the end of the last of the six novels under consideration in this study eloquently attests to Burroughs' metaphorical personification of the jungle:

Tarzan . . . saw the flowers close and open; he saw certain blooms which turned their faces always toward the sun; he saw leaves which moved when there was no breeze; he saw vines crawl like living things up the boles and over the branches of great trees; and to Tarzan of the Apes the flowers and the vines and the trees were living creatures. He often talked to them: as he talked to Goro, the moon, and Kudu, the sun, and always was he disappointed that they did not reply. He asked them questions; but they could not answer, though he knew that the whispering of the leaves was the language of the leaves—they talked with one another [6.180-181].

This passage pursues the idea of nature as animate with internal consistency and is equally consistent with this view as maintained throughout the entire corpus. Taken in its entirety as the most important landscape in all the books, the jungle is, of course, no mere metaphor but attains symbolic status.

Among the many narrative devices found in classical literature and used by Burroughs, the technique of the narrative within the narrative, as in Books 9–12 of the *Odyssey*, is fundamental. The entire Tarzan story is in effect a narrative within a narrative, for Burroughs is merely reporting an account that came from "dry official records of the British Colonial Office" and the "yellow, mildewed pages of a diary of a man long dead" (1.1).

Related to this device is that of connecting discrete elements of a larger narrative in a phrase or passage that picks up on an earlier one. This, too, reflects a Homeric approach. The linking feature of the narrative often involves suspense, which is created when an exciting event is interrupted by a digression or by the development of a parallel plot. For organization of the relationship among the interwoven plots, the link passage functions almost as a formal punctuation to the digression, saying in effect that the "main" narrative is once more at the center of the reader's attention. Although Burroughs particularly relies on this technique in the Martian series of novels in order to create complex and suspenseful plots, it is not lacking in the stories we are examining.

Let us consider some examples from *Return*. At the end of Chapter 12 (page 105), after skillfully constructing an atmosphere of impending doom for Tarzan, Burroughs has Tarzan quickly tossed overboard at night. The reader is eager to learn what will happen, but rather than pursue this particular twist in the novel's larger movement, Burroughs develops two subplots, merges them, and then separates them into a novel arrangement (pages 104–116). At the end of this development (page 116), a new crisis has been organized, but rather than continue with it, the author reverts to the earlier one, leaving the new one dangling. Thus, at page 116, as Jane, Clayton, and Thuran are left shipwrecked, alone, on the empty sea, the reader is whisked back to the end of Chapter 12 (page 105). The reader follows the further unfolding of Tarzan's narrative, momentarily forgetting the other one. A story within a story is, in a sense, now told, in which we learn how Tarzan came to know the Waziri and came to be their leader and chief. We know that he wants to make a trip to the fabled city of Opar for gold. But this story is interrupted by the gruesome account of the dying people in the drifting lifeboat (pages 150–159), which ends with an implication of imminent cannibalism (page 159). But, once more, the narrative view shifts back to Tarzan and his journey to Opar, filled as it is with marvels, horrors, and high adventure. This portion of the narrative concludes with Tarzan's incarceration in the "Chamber of the Dead, beneath the long-dead city of Opar" (2.174). The reader is now taken back to the story of Jane, Clayton, and Thuran (pages 175–183), which ends with the mechanically foreshadowing statement that "it was the next day that the great calamity befell" (2.183). Starting at page 183, the narrative with Tarzan at its center is reintroduced, and the weaving together of these two extended narratives with protagonists Tarzan and Jane, respectively, begins. The pattern here is one of amoeban interlinking that has been so thoroughly established that the confluence of the two discrete subplots into the mainstream of the novel appears quite natural for Burroughs' technique.

The sequence discussed may be represented schematically.

A ... 105   Tarzan thrown overboard ("he had been pitched over the low rail and was falling into the Atlantic")

B   105–116   Jane and Hazel meet, join each other, ship is wrecked; Jane in boat with Thuran, Clayton, and three sailors (they were alone in a small boat upon the broad Atlantic")

A   116–149   ("As Tarzan struck the water . . ."); Tarzan becomes chief of Waziri (". . . came into real kingship among men . . .")

B   150–159   ("Jane Porter had been the first of those in the lifeboat to awaken the morning after the wreck of the *Lady Alice*"); incipient cannibalism (". . . he lost consciousness")

A   160–174   ("The very night that Tarzan of the Apes became chief of the Waziri . . ."); journey to Opar ("She was gone,

and Tarzan of the Apes was left alone in the Chamber
of the Dead . . .")
B   175–183   ("Clayton dreamed that . . ."); rescue of a sort
A   183ff.   ("It was quite dark before La, the high priestess, returnec
to the Chamber of the Dead with food and drink for
Tarzan")

This brief example makes it quite obvious that the language
beginning and punctuating each section establishes the formal linkage
in such a way that a continuing series of narratives can be kept alive
side by side and constantly intermixed with each other. In this sense,
the technique permits the author not only to keep before the reader's
eye the relationship of the (at first) separate stories, but also to make
them "speak" to each other because of their persistent juxtaposition.
An important point throughout the development of these two narratives of Tarzan and Jane is the emerging and significant contrast
between the brutalization of the civilized and civilizing of the
primitive.

The type of interlinking observed in this section of *Return* is also
to be found in ancient literature. It involves the notion of a main, or
central, narrative which is constantly "interrupted" by various
digressions. This technique is basic in Homer. In drama one may
point, as just one example, to the meticulous organization of Aeschylus' play entitled *The Persians*, which, in a real sense, consists of
endless digressions from the slender main narrative that ostensibly
attempts to discern "'how the departed king, Xerxes, is faring."[4] Nor,
in this context, should one omit mention of the Greek historian
Herodotus or, for that matter, the Roman writer Julius Caesar who,
as we noted earlier, was well known to Burroughs in the Latin
original.[5]

Yet another narrative technique available to the author for
presenting his own "biased" view of a character or situation is the
so-called priamel, a corruption of the Latin *praeambulatio*, or a
"walk in front," a preface. The term refers quite specifically to the
listing of a series of prefatory statements or attributes against the
backdrop of which one is meant to view the final element in the
catalogue. Essentially a comparative device, this ancient technique
usually does two things. It calls attention to the final element as the
best or most important in the entire series, and it provides a con-

textual background whose specific elements may have some bearing on the understanding or interpretation of the last one. Conceived from the rhetorical point of view, the preface is auxetic, or enhancing, of the conclusion; in modern terms, it is the buildup. But, unlike a simple buildup, the prefatory terms of the priamel usually create a context within which the chief point acquires a highly specific importance.

As with so much in his language and technique, Burroughs also uses the priamel in a way that clearly recalls the classical prototypes. An obvious example appears early in *Tarzan*. Here the point is to demonstrate that Tarzan's movements were swift: "Quick was Sabor, the lioness, and quick were Numa and Sheeta, but Tarzan of the Apes was lightning" (1.63). The fact of his swiftness could well have been conveyed by the simple statement that "Tarzan was quick as lightning." But by expanding this comment and placing it in a context such as the priamel provides, Burroughs is able to make the reader appreciate this quality of his hero more pointedly. Tarzan is also defined partially in terms of the very animals, all swift, whom he excells in this particular ability. By itself, this priamel is merely an interesting application of an ancient technique, but after many such priamel views of Tarzan, or of any person or event, the reader or listener is led to formulate those attitudes and hold those opinions which the author wishes.

Return also defines Tarzan in terms of a beast in the following priamel which, it will be noted, is chiastic in its arrangement.

While it was yet light Tarzan came to a drinking place by the side of a jungle river. There was a ford there, and for countless ages the beasts of the forest had come down to drink at this spot. *Here* of a night might always be found either Sabor or Numa crouching in the dense foliage of the surrounding jungle awaiting an antelope or a water buck for their meal. *Here* came Horta, the boar, to water, and *here* came Tarzan of the Apes to make a kill, for he was very empty [2.119].

Tarzan is clearly linked to the animal world of which he is a part, and the implicit suggestion from the prefatory statements is that Tarzan is both a hunter of meat, as are Sabor or Numa, and a drinker of water, as is Horta. Tarzan's superiority over the animals, however, is strongly indicated by the chiastic arrangement of the whole, which sets Tarzan as an enclosing frame around them.

CHIASMUS	PRIAMEL
Tarzan	Here . . . Sabor or Numa
Sabor or Numa	Here . . . Horta
Horta	Here . . . Tarzan
Tarzan	

Once more, the mere fact of Tarzan's thirst and hunger could have been states without elaboration, but, wishing to enhance the stature of his hero at every possible turn of the narrative, Burroughs imparts the information in the context of the priamel. This device calls attention to the importance of Tarzan because he is the final element in the list, and it also makes it possible to see Tarzan as important in the larger context of nature.

In Chapter 1 of *Tales*, Tarzan for the first time becomes enamored of a female, but she is an ape. In the course of this chapter, Tarzan learns that for all the peoples of the jungle there are shes, but not for Tarzan.

"For the Gomangani there is another Gomangani," he said; "for Numa, the lion, there is Sabor, the lioness; for Sheeta there is a she of his own kind; for Bara, the deer; for Manu, the monkey; for all the beasts and the birds of the jungle is there a mate. Only for Tarzan of the Apes is there none. Taug is an ape. Teeka is an ape. Go back to Teeka. Tarzan is a man. He will go alone" [6.23].

This passage concludes, at least for the time being, the rivalry between Tarzan and Taug over Teeka, the she. Here the structure of the priamel allows both for the individual terms of comparison (Gomangani, lions, leopards, and so on) and the summarizing comparison ("all the beasts of the jungle"), the cumulative effect of which is to throw into high relief Tarzan's aloneness and singularity in this erotic jungle of his adolescence. The priamel effectively singles out Tarzan, makes of him something special, and in this way comments not only on the process of his maturation that is being explored in the entire book, but also on the heroic mold in which the author is casting him. Aloneness, apartness, difference—these are all the essential hallmarks of the heroic individual in Homeric literature and among the protagonists of classical tragedy.

The priamel provides a definite point of view about Tarzan and his distinctness from the apes. This distinctness, from a somewhat altered vantage, recurs in the last chapter of *Tales*, where it is part of the larger ring composition that informs the entire book. The actual material of this priamel is picked up a bit later (6.67), with much the same effect.

In Chapter 1 Tarzan's apartness is delineated in terms of his not having a mate; here (6.67) it is in terms of not having a child. As a *Bildungsroman*, this book may be said to have moved from dwelling on the protagonist's incipient stirrings of the sensation of love to the unequivocally adult desire for offspring. Although there will be a more detailed discussion of this point in chapter 4, the general parallels to the larger movement of Homer's *Odyssey*, with its child-adult pair Telemachus-Odysseus, should not go unnoticed at this time.

The preoccupation with his status as a loner and an individual who does not fit the normative pattern of his given society reveals Tarzan once more in the same light as the Homeric hero and those of the Attic tragedians and the comic poet Aristophanes. There can hardly be a question of the fortuitous use of the priamel in these passages, for they are too consistently employed in those instances in which Tarzan evaluates himself in relation to the world he inhabits.

No attempt has been made in this chapter to present an exhaustive analysis of all the techniques Burroughs had at his command. Only the more common and more obviously successful ones, especially as they are related to prototypes in the classical literatures, have been analyzed here.

In using the narrative techniques discussed in the present chapter and the stylistic features treated in chapter 1, Burroughs declares himself a member of good standing in the long tradition of heroic literature that, for us, begins with the Homeric epics. Burroughs' masterly adaptations of various techniques from the epics of Greece and Rome underscore and sustain this powerful sense of the heroicness of the world and the action he in turn has created.

ANIMALS

___3___

The community of apes is never just a community of apes in Burroughs; there is always an implied comparison, however slight, to what is usually called civilized society. It is not that the perfections of ape society are numberless, nor that the world of the apes is without blemish, but rather that human society, both African black and European white, is most starkly prominent in all its short-comings (as Burroughs saw it) when set off against the "natural" order of the apes. The intensity of this synkrisis of societies is vigorously impressed upon the reader in the opening chapters of the first novel, *Tarzan*.

We first encounter the civilized world when we learn that Tarzan's future parents are to set off to Africa in order that his father may undertake "a thorough investigation of the unfair treatment of black British subjects by the officers of a friendly European power" (1.2). The circumstances that prompt Lord Greystoke's journey to Africa do not, it seems, speak well for that civilized world from which he comes and of which England is a part. Nor, as the narrative sweeps along, is one's confidence in the rational and civilized behavior of human beings increased by the description of the good ship *Fuwalda*, a type of craft with "crews composed of the offscourings of the sea— unhanged murderers and cutthroats of every race and every nation. . . . Her officers were swarthy bullies, hating and hated by their crew. The captain . . . was a brute in his treatment of his men" (1.3).

Before we have even met any animals in the zoological sense of the word, we have been introduced to a feral sampling of humanity. Events that subsequently take place on the *Fuwalda* are a kind of microcosm of the utter ineffectiveness of the appeals of civilization (the Greystokes) to the naked drives of uncontrolled human passion. The brutal death of the brutal captain (1.11) signals a breakdown of order; even the savage leader of the crew finds it difficult to control his unruly men. The only factor mitigating this unhappy impression of human beastliness is the leader's feeble display of gratitude towards the Greystokes for having prevented the captain from shooting him. Finally, the heroic efforts of the civilized John Clayton, Lord Greystoke, to carve out a society for himself, his wife, and newborn son in the jungle are not without serious and indeed fatal inadequacies.

After this graphic portrayal has exposed the flawed ways of all levels of human society, we cut, almost as if the medium were film, to the ape society of Kerchak.

In the forest of the table-land a mile back from the ocean old Kerchak the ape was on a rampage of rage among his people.

The younger and lighter members of his tribe scampered to the higher branches of the great trees to escape his wrath; risking their lives upon the branches that scarce supported their weight rather than face old Kerchak in one of his fits of uncontrolled anger [1.27].

Given the preceding variations of man's world, we have no great difficulty in making the connection with the apes' world. How different is the raging Kerchak from the brutish captain of the *Fuwalda*? from the giant Black Michael? from the nameless politicians of a "friendly European power" (1.2) that tolerates the brutalization of human beings?

At line 493 in the first book of the *Iliad*, Homer cuts from the human world of the Greeks at Troy to the heights of Mount Olympus, where the quarrel of the gods partially recapitulates that of the humans. Serious argument did take place among the gods, but a reconciliation was effected, and none of the calamitous events ensuing among men came about in the divine world. One is forced to conclude that Homer wanted his audience to draw from this synkrisis the appropriate inferences that the human solution was not a very clever one.

There are two important points in Burroughs' case: (1) Kerchak's madness passes when the baby dies. (2) Instead of confronting the enraged Kerchak, "the other males scattered in all directions" (1.27). In short, although damage is done, it stops long before the whole society is whisked up in the destructive impulses of ungovernable rage. The apes, by contrast with the humans, seem to have found a rational way of dealing with the irrational so that the society is preserved without serious disruptions.

Of course, the naturalistic or zoological accuracy in Burroughs' depiction of ape society is of no more consequence to us than is the theological veracity of Homer's presentation of deity. Homer was no more a theologian than Burroughs was a zoologist; both deploy their nonhuman actors the better to explain and comment on the human participants.

In this comparison of apes and men, we initially favor the apes. The impression is reinforced on many later occasions by this same typical passage in which an ape goes berserk, only to be avoided by the other members of the tribe. Without confrontation to fuel them, such sudden seizures spend themselves of their own accord; if confrontation becomes necessary, a single death may follow, but the society endures unharmed. The latter alternative takes place when Tarzan destroys his foster father (1.55f.), as well as when Tarzan finally kills Kerchak to become the leader of the tribe (1.85). Repetition is the best way to drive a point home, and these descriptions of the essentially safe way in which the apes handle "those strange, wild fits of insane rage which attacks the males of many of the fiercer animals of the jungle" (1.51) serve as sustained foil to the more ruinous consequences of rage among men. In the society of the apes anger is, as with the Homeric gods, self-limiting; in both Homer and Burroughs, among men, it tends to involve the larger group beyond the stricken individual. Although it is impossible to know if Burroughs consciously modeled his opening sequence about humans and the tribe of Kerchak on the opening of Homer's *Iliad*, it is a fact that both begin with a synkristic study of the personal and social consequences of anger. It is a heroic theme of venerable antiquity.

A rather detailed account of an ape community can be assembled from the scattered references in the first six novels. The associations and behavior which Burroughs assigns to his apes are not based on the ethologist's observations but on those of the writer working in a recognizable tradition. There are more than a few points of contact between Burroughs' generalizations about the society of the anthropoids and that of the anthropomorphic gods of Homer and other writers in antiquity.

The great apes are subject to a single, authoritarian patriarch whose rule is based on his power. Only when he becomes too weak relative to some younger bull can he be defeated, but until that time his sway is supreme. Typical is the incumbency of the crusty old tyrant Kerchak who has successfully defended himself against both foreign attack and internal revolt.

One of the set scenes in the depiction of the anthropoid community is the struggle of a younger ape to kill an older leader and himself assume the mantle of kingship. This battle of the generations is, of course, a familiar pattern from Greek myth, in particular as it is presented in Hesiod's *Theogony*. In a series of great battles between the generations, Hesiod at last has Zeus, the youngest of the gods in his generation, overthrow his tyrannical father Kronos and become king of the gods.

The mechanism for achieving kingship in a community is as explicitly delineated for Burroughs' apes as it is for the gods in the Greek account of Hesiod. Apes, like the gods, must have the social stability that is ultimately based on the autocrat's physical and mental prowess. And an autocrat, anthropomorphic deity as well as humanized anthropoid, may certainly be benevolent in the execution of his duties. As the gods are both idealizations and replicas of mortal imperfections, so the apes live a life that in its primitiveness is both a romantic idyll beside the corruptions of man's world and an unfortunate image of his less noble instincts. Indeed, the despotic autocrat will soon find himself in trouble, as the great ape Terkoz discovers (1.152). Zeus is no different in this respect.

The family organization of the apes is unmistakably patriarchal, a feature they share with the divine families. There is never a serious question about the patriarchal nature of the Olympian household, nor is there even a hint that the apes tolerate anything else. But like

coquettish goddesses, the female apes can elicit predictable reactions
from males who would fight over them, as is clear from the episode
involving lovely Teeka and the young rivals Taug and Tarzan
(6.9ff.). A female can get her way simply by being considered too
valuable to interfere with, since she might just leave the tribe for
another. This is the case with Kala, the she-ape who adopts Tarzan as
her own. Her husband, Tublat, distressed at the slow progress the
strange infant is making, insists that Kala abandon him. Kala refuses,
and Tublat takes his problems to the leader. But Kerchak's intercession is futile. Kala gets her way.

The obstreperous female is a familiar figure in the Olympian world,
and none is more obstreperous than Hera, wife of Zeus. The apes,
like the deities, have on occasion to contend with a difficult she
who can make life miserable for a bull. Teeka, for example, is so hard
to manage for the bull who abducted her that he concludes he made
a mistake in taking her (6.155).

But for all the idyll and fundamentally carefree life the apes live,
there is, as among the gods, continual squabbling in which lies the
potential for the dissolution of the tribe (1.91). Even the famous
council scenes on Olympus find their counterpart among the apes.
Allusion to such councils is made in Tales (6.119, and cf. 1.152), and
specific mention comes in connection with the Dum-Dum, the
supreme ceremony of ape society (4.66). Indeed, in one passage we
are explicitly told that the sequestered and sheltered area in which
the ceremony of the Dum-Dum takes place is "the council chamber
of the great apes" (2.190).

Burroughs' groups of apes do differ from the Olympian household
in certain respects. For example, there is only one Olympian household, but clearly a number of tribal groups of apes vie for supremacy
within a given region. In general, the gods, as well as the goddesses,
have few scruples about sexual promiscuity. As a norm of behavior,
this pattern is lacking among the apes because their social life is in
fact polygamous (cf. 3.24). Yet, one infers (cf. 1.153ff., 4.76) that
a neighbor's mate is not coveted or molested under normal circumstances. That Burroughs did not create his apes in the promiscuous
mold of the Grek divinities is more than compensated for by the
lurid, violent, and at times aggressive eroticism that is the hallmark
of Burroughs' love scenes.

In the divine world little is made of the needs of offspring. Such second-generation deities as Hermes and Athena, for example, are considered part of the adult population on Olympus; they are neither helpless nor in need of parental protection. Burroughs patterns the relationship of anthropoid parent to child on the human counterpart. The young are quite helpless and must be looked after by the whole community; the harrowing incidents involving the offspring of Teeka and Taug, Gazan, show the genuine sense of solidarity among the group and responsibility by the parents (6.61f., 148ff., 1.45, 3.32).

The food and drink of the gods is rather limited, consisting primarily of ambrosia and nectar. When they visit human habitations, however, they partake of the variegated foods of their hosts. The description of food in Homer belongs to the category of set scenes, in which the predictable dishes and their preparation are recited. The apes have a greatly varied diet compared to that of the gods, and the various items are paraded in the scenes that describe their feeding. Among the delicacies that sustain them are bananas, beetles, birds, bugs, caterpillars, cabbage palm, eggs, field mice, fruits, fungi, gray plums, grubs, grubworms, herbs, insects, mammals, meat, nuts, pisang, reptiles, rodents, scitamine, wild pineapple, and even human flesh. The list is perhaps more Aristophanic than Homeric in its alimentary fullness.

As discussed in Chapter 1, the clusters of vocabulary used to delineate the jungle and its aspects are limited and, to a certain extent, predictable. This usage of epithets, so common in Homeric epic, is also associated with the presentation of certain characters in Burroughs (for example, Tarzan, Jane, civilized man) and animals (for example, apes). For in his adaptation of animals, especially the great apes, as the typological equivalents of the deities in ancient literature, Burroughs uses a narrowly characterizing set of epithets in descriptive elaboration of them.

From just the first book, *Tarzan*, the following generalizations about the physical nature of the apes stand out: great, huge, grotesque, ferocious, powerful, fierce, awesome, fearsome, and large. These are standard epithets applied with almost automatic regularity to the apes, and they acquire the force of conventional formulas. Among other common attributives, many of which address themselves to the physical appearance of the apes, are hairy, shaggy, hideous, sullen, brooding, and snarling. A favorite substantival appellation is the word "brute." In addition to these generalizations, an extensive vocabulary, highly formulaic and specific in its applicability, is devoted to the description of individual parts of the apes' anatomy from head to toe. Their brows, for example, are shaggy (1.16, 5.153) and beetling (4.68, 6.73); their eyes, more fully described than most of the physical features, are close-set (1.16, 28), wicked (1.57, 5.115), bloodshot (1.28, 3.33), and savage (4.67, 6.46); and their fangs are mighty (1.156, 3.106), great (1.55, 6.73), powerful (1.36, 4.33), long (4.48, 6.46), sharp (1.58, 6.118), bared (1.33, 3.127), fighting (3.33, 6.183), and yellow (4.76, 5.43). Of all the vast numbers of epithets applied to the bodies of the apes, the most widely applied is "hairy." This persistent epithet is attached to the following parts of the body: face (5.97), chin (4.90), throat (3.23), neck (1.33), arms (4.65), hands (6.42), paws (1.53), limbs (5.98), legs (6.40), body (1.154), coat (6.20), shoulders (4.86), chest (3.23), breast (6.46), back (4.77), and stomach (5.43).

Here Burroughs merely follows in the tradition of the Homeric epic when he develops a repetitive vocabulary for the apes (or for Tarzan, or villains, or lions, and so forth). It is part of the stylistic coloring that makes Burroughs' novels into a recognizably traditional narrative of epic achievement. Why, it may be asked, is there such an emphasis on the hairiness of the apes? Does Homer use a comparable favorite epithet for the gods? For like the individual deities, the collective of gods also was given fixed epithets by Homer and his tradition. As a group they are called, among other things, dwellers on Olympus, blessed, heavenly, deathless, and always-existing. The last two epithets are extremely common in both the *Iliad* and *Odyssey*, and the adjective "deathless" in Greek means "god." One may speculate that the popularity of those two phrases, both of which address themselves to a quintessential distinction between gods and men, namely, the mortality of man and the immortality of divinity, arises from the deep conviction of Greek culture that impassable boundaries must be maintained between man and god. Deathlessness and eternal existence define the essential difference between the two orders of beings as effectively and unmistakably as possible.

In Burroughs there is a severe distinction between the worlds of man and of animals, and it is only Tarzan who, like the semidivine heroes of classical literature and myth, can straddle the two worlds. Since apes are not immortal, some other distinguishing appellative is called for, and where Homer goes to an internal and almost philosophical source for establishing difference, Burroughs is content—and perhaps his sense of auctorial humor has been given free play here— to restrict himself to external and easily visible differences. At any rate, it is significant that the first time we, along with Tarzan, are made aware of a distinction between man and ape, the cardinal point on which the discovery of that difference hinges is precisely the matter of hairiness as opposed to hairlessness.

He was nearly ten before he commenced to realize that a great difference existed between himself and his fellows. His little body, burned brown by exposure, suddenly caused him feelings of intense shame, for he realized that it was entirely hairless, like some low snake, or other reptile [1.35].

Much is made of Tarzan's other disfiguring marks—tiny split of a mouth, puny teeth, pinched nose, blank whiteness of his eyes, and so forth—in comparison to the distinctively red eyes of the apes, their broad, flat noses, long fangs, and great lips. But it is their hairiness which seems to set them off against Tarzan with finality. A similar point is made in *Tales*, when Tarzan is competing with his former childhood friend, the now adult Taug, for the affections of lovely Teeka. Tarzan comes to the unhappy conclusion that he cannot compete on equal terms with the handsome Taug, a jungle Narcissus infatuated with his own charms.

Taug grunted, for there was no comparison. How could one compare his beautiful coat with the smooth and naked hideousness of Tarzan's bare hide? Who could see beauty in the stingy nose of the Tarmangani after looking at Taug's broad nostrils? And Tarzan's eyes? Hideous things, showing white about them, and entirely unrimmed with red. Taug knew that his own bloodshot eyes were beautiful, for he had seen them reflected in the glassy surface of many a drinking pool [6.16].

It is not that Burroughs fails to play these scenes for the element of humor, but there is also a serious point here, as in the distinctions between men and gods in ancient literature. In ancient literature, however, there is none of the emerging idea that it is the human hero rather than the nonhuman actor who is dominant and superior. Burroughs has taken a traditional distinction and made something different of it within the context of the conventions in which he is writing. For Tarzan, unlike the heroes of ancient literature, is shown to be infinitely superior to the animals. It is his man's mind, his human intellect, which always triumphs over the greater physical strength of the beasts. No ancient hero, of course, ever for long holds the upper hand over the gods, since their physical and mental power, along with their immortality, makes them infinitely preeminent among men. Where the ancient writers made clear the inferiority of the hero to that world of divinity to which he was always striving, Burroughs develops a hero who, coming from the Darwinian world of apes from which all men come, has surpassed their status and is their superior.

This development reveals not only Burroughs' awareness of and participation in an heroic tradition, but also his innovating departure from it. He makes the tradition work for him without being trapped in a mindless replication of it. Where the ancients wanted to believe there was something divine, or at least the possibility for it, in man, Burroughs keeps reminding us of our zoological phylogeny. Both the ancient writers and Burroughs are true to their respective eras. Hesiod's *Theogony* and *Catalogue of Women* established a more or less direct provenience of men from divinity, and many other writers of antiquity believed, at least for artistic purposes, in this "fact" of man's origin. Like so many of his contemporaries and our own, Burroughs was deeply impressed with Darwin's theory of evolution,[1] and from that cultural vantage he could not help seeing something of the beast in man's background. One's own prejudices or inclinations will determine whether it is to be deemed better to be descended from gods or from beasts. In any event, the ancient gods behave bestially at times, and Burroughs' beasts are not beyond behavior we might consider divine in its self-sacrifice and compassion (for example, Kala, the ape mother who adopts Tarzan; Taug and Teeka; and Tantor the elephant).

The emotional life of the apes in general shows remarkable similarities to that of human beings, and the likeness, as likeness, is strongly reminiscent of the gods in ancient literature. Thus, the apes can be vengeful (1.29, 6.149), filled with sorrow (4.59), given to grand hatreds (6.121, 6.187), and preoccupied by fear (3.38, 5.100f.), but they are also capable of showing the opposite range of emotions, such as maternal love (6.61), sexual love (6.23), friendship (3.33), and loyalty (6.186). These very human failings and strengths are also well developed in some of the divinities of ancient literature. Athena's friendship for Odysseus, Zeus' gratitude to Thetis, Poseidon's hatred of Odysseus and his desire for revenge on him, Ares' fear that drives him from the battlefield in great haste—these are some examples that come to mind.

The apes, like the gods, have been humanized.

Psychological characterization in the clinical framework to which all of us who live in a post-Freudian and post-Jungian world are accustomed was, of course, not possible in antiquity. One does not find in ancient literature those narrative digressions in which the author steps back from his created world to examine clinically its inner workings and psychological relationships, for the critical vocabulary and psychological categories that are so familiar to us today were not yet in existence. Of the many modern disciplines which have firm roots in antiquity, psychology is conspicuous by its absence. It is easy to name names of ancients who wrote works or were active in such fields as medicine, music, architecture, pottery, statecraft, physics, philosophy, astronomy, and others, but not a single psychologist. Psychology or psychological awareness of human behavior, however, was most definitely not lacking among the ancients. Some of the great writers of antiquity were at least as perceptive as any modern author or clinician about the byways of human motivations. And their "language" was, in short, the divine world.

The Greek gods were well established in the culture and, over centuries and perhaps millennia, had acquired relatively fixed characters, predictable patterns of behavior, exclusive spheres of influence and power, and recognizable attributes. They had become a kind of culturally determined symbol. If one considers an example like the goddess Athena, the process will perhaps become clear. The discussion of Athena is applicable, with appropriate shifts, to any deity we meet in ancient literature, and what the gods tend to be in ancient literature, both as characters and as psychological realities, the animals tend to be in Burroughs' world.

An author who uses Athena as a persona in a narrative can and will rely on the "given" in her character, those overlays and associations which she might automaticaly evoke simply by being the goddess Athena. Since there is more than a hint of the helper in her personality, it is quite reasonable that she should appear as an aid and supporter of her favorites. Simultaneously, living a code that demands help for friends and harm to enemies, she can prove a wrathful and devastating opponent to those who oppose her favorites. Clearly, Odysseus in the *Odyssey* capitalizes on her fondness for him, and the suitors of Odysseus' wife become the unhappy objects of her less benign attentions. Her role in this connection may perhaps be seen as revealing her more fundamental task of maintaining the integrity of society, in this case the home of Odysseus. At any rate, Athena's relationship to Odysseus and his foes underlines a general pattern that is frequently encountered in the associations between a given deity and mortal or semimortal. The deity helps the human and his friends, but harms his enemies.

But are we, or were the listeners of Homer's performances, to assume that the epiphany of an Athena is to be taken literally? Who, or what, is Athena? Because of her inordinately practical and prudent view of the best way to manage life's contingencies, the poet is pressing these attributes and characteristics of the goddess into service *as a means for talking not about Athena but about Odysseus.* Athena has here become a kind of physical externalization of inner processes in the evaluating and calculating mind of Odysseus.

In the first book of the *Iliad,* a not dissimilar role is assigned to Athena. At that point in the narrative, the leader of the Greek army, Agamemnon, and the greatest fighter among the Greeks who assembled at Troy, Achilles, have reached an apparent impasse in an argument involving a young woman and their respective sense of honor and glory before the other Greeks. Achilles, in a towering rage, is about to pull his sword and slay the insufferable Agamemnon. The action in the narrative breaks off on the mortal plane, and Homer informs us that Athena, in consultation with the goddess Hera, made a hasty trip down from Mount Olympus to the Greek camp on the Trojan plain. Here she appeared *only* to Achilles; Homer is quite explicit that no other person saw her as she appeared amid the assembled Greeks. Nonetheless, she and Achilles hold a long conversation in which Athena appeals to the more rational part of Achilles' character. She points out to him that, if he will defray such present gratification as he might derive from killing Agamemnon, his long-range profit will be increased tenfold. The hero's anger subsides, for even in his uncontrollable rage he is shrewd enough to appreciate the unassailable logic of Athena's pragmatic appeal. He therefore sheathes the sword, controls his anger, and allows his opponent Agamemnon to live. Because of the clear stage directions with which Homer engineers this encounter, one can hardly take Athena as anything but a graphic externalization of the powerful profit (in whatever coin) motive in Achilles that speaks to the calculating rationality in his makeup.[2] Again, as in the case of Odysseus, it is the rationality, not the femaleness, of the goddess that is of primary importance in this relationship between herself and the hero.

In a much later writer from antiquity, the Latin poet Ovid, we meet the irrational component in the rational Athena. In a story in his long narrative poem the *Metamorphosis*, Ovid presents us with Athena not as the externalization of any human irrationality or madness, but as herself subject to a grand fit of uncontrollable rage. The story in question treats her contest with the mortal girl Arachne (*Metamorphoses* 6.1ff.). In addition, other stories point up this less reasonable aspect of the goddess. In short, inherent in the accepted biography of Athena is the possibility for either type of behavior, a prudent calculation of self-interest or a totally irrational abandoning of reasoned behavior. The polar extremes, ready-made in the traditional understanding of the goddess, lend themselves to auctorial exploitation in the elucidation of character and narrative.

One other feature of the literary Athena as an hypostatization of human aspirations should be mentioned here, for it has a bearing on both the *Odyssey* and our ultimate point of connection, the world of Burroughs. No reader of the *Odyssey* can forget the important role Athena plays for Telemachus, the son of Odysseus, as well as for Odysseus himself. It will be recalled that at the opening of the *Odyssey*, Telemachus is contemplating making a journey to find his father, now some twenty years gone. Telemachus himself would be about twenty years old at this time, and as a young man he has some difficulty deciding on proper behavior and action. Athena, in the shape of a mortal, the old family friend Mentes, advises the young man on his proper course of action. After Telemachus gathers up the courage to decide about his future and announces he will embark on a journey in search of his father, Athena again appears, this time in the guise of Mentor, to help promote his voyage. As Mentor, Athena is assigned the role of helping to educate Telemachus to become a man, to become a responsible adult in the world in which he lives.

The discussion of the narratives involving Athena and some mortal could equally well have dealt with some other deity and favorite (or hated) mortals. The pattern of divine help or obstruction towards friend or foe in the human world is a pervasive one in ancient literature. At an even more general level, we are no doubt familiar with the extensively documented appearance of helping and hindering animals, gnomes, trolls, and fairy-like figures in the folklore of nearly all world cultures. The use of the gods in ancient literature to fulfill this function (although animals are also so utilized) is perhaps a variation of a basic pattern. This suggestion is supported by the ease with which all the deities of the anthropomorphic Greek and Roman pantheons change from human to animal shape and vice versa. Some gods are more adept at this transformation than others, but all have some relationship to the world of animals, whether by actual incarnation or because of animal "mascots" that are associated with or accompany them. The gods are not only anthropomorphic but also theriomorphic.

This background, though brief, is sufficient for an examination of Burroughs' adaptation of the divine world in ancient epic to the animals in the world of Tarzan. A definite and rather carefully maintained parallelism exists in the operation of the two worlds. The emphasis here is on adaptation, not adoption. An indiscriminate arrogation of features from an earlier tradition into his own work can only lead an author into dead ends. Only when he makes something new of the old, without at the same time destroying the old or obfuscating the new, is an author being most traditional and most evocative of the earlier world of thought and experience on which he is drawing in order to define his own.

This caveat is desirable lest some construe that the animals in Burroughs *are* the gods; they obviously are not. But in the psychological dimension the worlds of Olympian gods and jungle animals are most alike, and it is this aspect of divinity in ancient literature which Burroughs has exploited. But just as deities are in their own right characters and actors in the epic or drama in which they are found, so, too, the animals in Burroughs are frequently individualized and made to play out their own roles. And as the Olympian family, with its virtues as well as its many defects, is always at least an implicit parallel to the human world, so the familial and social activities of animals appear always to be involved to some extent in the world of Tarzan and other men. The synkrisis of god-man is common in Homer; the synkrisis of man-animal and their respective societies is frequent in Burroughs. As Homeric, tragic, Vergilian, and other deities constantly help or hinder the humans, so the animals in Tarzan's world help friends and harm foes. (A core theme of *Beasts* is clearly predicated on this classical precept of popular ethics.) As the gods become a kind of magnifying glass through which the humans may be seen more accurately, the animals also permit the reader to gain insight into the psychological and spiritual workings of humans and their relationships with each other.

The literate reader will not have worked his way far into *Son* before the unmistakable sense of *déjà lu*, as it were, begins to assert itself. This story has indeed been told earlier. Its first known appearance is in the *Odyssey* of Homer, in which the central characters of the narrative are Telemachus, Athena, Penelope, Peisistratos, and Odysseus. On his journey Telemachus is helped, inspired, and taught by Athena to speak as a man among the men and households he visits, to learn the ways of the aristocratic society to which he belongs, and in brief, to handle himself as an adult. Athena is representative of that molding influence or force within the individual and his society which transforms the child into the matured adult. This rite of passage from one estate to another, like those of birth, marriage, and death, is fundamental among humankind and is firmly entrenched in the Western consciousness from the archetypal account of the *Odyssey*. The child comes to recognize, as Athena puts it to Telemachus, that "in no way should you have childish ways, for no longer are you a child" (*Odyssey* 1.296f.). A symbolically powerful way for the son to assert his independence from the protective mother is to declare that independence openly. Telemachus unequivocally makes the point to his mother, Penelope.

But go into the house and take care of your own affairs, the loom and
shuttle, and give your servants orders to attend the work. Talk shall be the
concern of the men, all of them, but especially me. For mine is the power in
the household [*Odyssey* 1.355 ff].

The inspirations of Athena are the poetic externalizations of the
maturing process within Telemachus, and in using the goddess to
make these events concrete, the poet is able to account for the inculca-
tion of personal and communal values in the young man. As goddess,
Athena is well suited to this role, for she is a goddess not only of
wisdom, but also, in origin, of social cohesiveness. Furthermore, she
is an old friend of the father, Odysseus.

What has all of this to do with Burroughs' *Son*? Burroughs' story
is the same basic narrative, for it describes the education of the young
man to the ways of the adult world. Burroughs does not make a
one-for-one transference from Homer but rather always makes
changes and shifts emphases. Some background is necessary. In the
book before *Son*, *Beasts*, the apeman had gathered around himself a
crew of animals under his personal control. Among them was the
great ape Akut, whom Tarzan had once spared from death and so
made into a lasting friend (3.25ff.), and by the end of *Beasts* a genuine
and enduring friendship has developed between the man and the
animal. At the start of *Son*, the ape has become the property of
Tarzan's ancient foe, Paulvitch. By a concatenation of circumstances,
the son of Tarzan and Akut become involved in a series of escapades
that end in their traveling to Africa, where events force them to take
flight into the jungle (4.35). Only years later is the son at last reunited
with his parents but then as an adult in his own right. This *Bildungsroman* concludes, as all good romantic comedy should, with a
wedding reaffirming social wholeness and continuity, a point that
evokes multiple associations not only with the *Odyssey* but also with
other Tarzan novels.

Akut the ape, or Ajax, as he has been dubbed (4.13), plays the role
of pedagogue to Jack, the son of Tarzan. Here Akut plays Mentor to
Jack's Telemachus. Mentor, the old friend of Odysseus, twenty years
previously had been entrusted with the care of the entire household.
Akut, too, as we have seen, has a friendship of long standing with

Tarzan. The events of *Beasts* are precipitated by the supposed kidnapping of the infant Jack, still tiny enough to be wheeled about in a carriage by a nurse (3.9); at the start of *Son*, Jack is in his pre- or early teens, and considerable time has elapsed since the conclusion of *Beasts*. Furthermore, Akut is specifically said to be "old . . . but if his age had impaired his physical or mental powers in the slightest it was not apparent" (4.13). Akut the animal functions in the same role as Athena the goddess in the *Odyssey*, for both Akut and Athena guide their respective self-adopted charges in the journey to adulthood.

It is interesting that Athena is not the only guide who disguises herself. The first time we meet her, she appears as Mentes (*Odyssey* 1.105), but her main disguise in her relationship with Telemachus and the mortals about him is that of Mentor. Nor is Telemachus unaware that he is being given directions by a divine presence that can teach him what he does not know about the world (*Odyssey* 1.420, 2.262, 2.297). Jack is, of course, fully aware of Akut as an animal, but Burroughs seems to have wanted to introduce this important motif of the "divinity (or animal) disguised," if only in a narrative context. The fact is that the ape must be disguised for the journey from London to Africa, so that Jack and Akut appear as "a youth accompanying his invalid grandmother, [who] boarded a steamer at Dover. The old lady was heavily veiled, and so weakened by age and sickness that she had to be wheeled aboard the vessel in an invalid chair" (4.30). Akut's disguise does not serve precisely the same purpose as Athena's, but both are transformed to prevent other humans from recognizing their nonhumanness. One might also note the possibility of a conscious inversion of the prototypical relationship. In Homer, the female goddess Athena is disguised as the male Mentor; in Burroughs, the male animal Akut is disguised as the female grandmother.

At the start of the *Odyssey*, Telemachus is openly exploited by the suitors who are eating him out of his future inheritance. The youth is caught in the middle of old enmities and jealousies between Odysseus and other important households on the island of Ithaca. Athena is trying to extricate Telemachus from involvement and to protect him from the deadly scheming of the suitors (*Odyssey* 4.663ff., 842ff.). It is, therefore, interesting to find that Jack has been placed in the middle of ancient hatreds between Tarzan and the Russian villain, Paulvitch. Again, Burroughs seems to have applied the Odyssean pattern in such a way that no serious doubt about the intended parallelism may be entertained. And there is more.

Just as Athena, in the preparations in *Odyssey* 20 and 21, and in the execution in *Odyssey* 22, is the nonhuman instrument of the vengeance that is exacted from the enemies of Telemachus' father, so, too, Akut the ape proves to be both instrument and agent of the death that finally meets Paulvitch, the enemy of Jack's father (4.28ff.). The suitors have also plotted violence against Telemachus himself, and for this, too, as well as the harm done Odysseus, they are punished with death. This feature is paralleled by Burroughs in the account of the American thief Condon, who tries to rob Jack and his "grandmother" but is instead killed for his efforts by Akut. Just as the father Odysseus has always been helped out of difficulties by the guiding presence of Athena, so the son Telemachus finds in the goddess a comfort and an inspirer of confidence; and just as the father Tarzan was helped by Akut in *Beasts*, so the son Jack has discovered in the protective presence of the ape not only consolation against his sense of loss of his parents, but also a lifesaving companion for his journey.

Furthermore, Telemachus and Athena (disguised as Mentor) leave the island of Ithaca for his journey and do so on a boat with companions (*Odyssey* 2.399 ff.); Jack and Akut (disguised as the grandmother) leave the island of Britain and do so by steamer in the company of other travelers and a well-disposed crew (4.30).

Penelope was very reluctant to let Telemachus go on his trip (*Odyssey* 2.374ff.),and even his nurse did not take kindly to the plan (*Odyssey* 2.363ff.). This pattern of the mother (or mother-figure) who attempts to prevent the child from doing what he must in order to express his independence and growing sense of himself as an individual is also very prominent in *Son*. Jack's mother is quite concerned about the direction her son's interests are taking, for she fears he is falling too much under the influence of his father's former way of life. Like Penelope-Eurycleia with Telemachus, Jane makes a strong effort (4.15f.) to prevent the son from following in the footsteps of the father. Jack is not, of course, setting out in search of his father, but the underlying dynamics of his effort to break free and fulfill his heredity by doing as his father, Tarzan, did are identical, as a kind of psychological odyssey, to the one Telemachus undertakes. For Telemachus the traveler is living up to the pattern of his widely traveling father, and although the language of Homer is not that of the genetic heritage to which Jane (and Tarzan in his reply to her) alludes, Homer nonetheless has the same point in mind when he has Athena-as-Mentes say to Telemachus: "But come, tell me this and speak to the point, if you are really the son of Odysseus himself, big as you are. Your head and your fine eyes look terribly like his—and we were together a great deal before he went off to Troy . . ." (*Odyssey* 1.206–210). In both Homer and Burroughs, the mothers try to hold the son back. But in each case ontogeny will out and the bloodline will tell, and the nonhuman actor is the agent of the final transformation, the goddess Athena for Telemachus and the beast Akut for Jack.

Given Burroughs' great indebtedness, documented in the two previous chapters, to the ancient tradition in both language and technique, undeniably there are striking parallels between the opening of Homer's *Odyssey* and Burroughs' *Son*. Burroughs' debt to Homer is manifest not merely in the general development of the notion of a young man's education into adulthood, but also in what we have just seen to be the detailed particulars of Burroughs' adaptation of the ancient prototype. Jack's education, like Telemachus', recapitulates the father's growth, and in both cases their education comes through nonhuman agents. Akut's role is a prime example of the notion that animals in Burroughs' works function as typological equivalents of the gods in ancient literature. Both externalize human motives, desires, and perceptions.

Apparently, the humanization of the gods fulfilled some deeply felt need of the ancients. One might argue that making the gods human brings them closer to humanity and divests them of that fearsome mystery that characterized deity in contemporary cultures of the ancient Near East. For whatever reasons, the Greeks had greater need to make the gods like themselves, and so perhaps more accessible and comprehensible, than any previous culture had. It could also be argued that demystification of deity is but another way of making men more like the gods.

The Homeric heroes had a strong impulse to be god-like, as the common use of such epithets as "god-like" in application to men indicates. At the same time, it was undesirable to be like a god. The paradox, or central problem, as Guthrie calls it in his illuminating discussion of this dilemma,[3] lies in the coupling of the intense striving for god-like stature with the forceful interdiction against hybristic desires to equal the gods. The great man, the hero, must somehow bridge this essentially unbridgeable chasm between being god-like and not being god-like. The hero, in the technical sense of that word, is already halfway to heaven, for one of his parents is divine, but he will never fully get there, except in the extraordinarily rare case of someone like Heracles.

Apparently, the mingling of man and god in ancient literature held out a kind of paradigm of what *could* happen, of the potential inherent in a truly unique human being for somehow participating in the divine. To the Greeks of the archaic period, this kind of exaltation of the possibilities for man seems to have been a necessary antidote to their otherwise pervasive and overwhelming pessimism regarding the meagreness of man and his problematical destiny in the larger scheme of things. In short, one might simplify to a degree and think of the exaltation of man's possibilities as a kind of psychological mechanism to compensate for a pessimistic assessment of his perceived reality.

But the humanization of the apes can hardly be explained on the same basis that is suggested here for the humanization of the gods. Although Burroughs obviously offers the notion that there is much of the beast in man and much of man in the beast, he is not suggesting that there is both an impulse in man that makes him want to be like the great anthropoids and a prohibition against such a presumptuous wish. Rather, the anthropomorphic anthropoids in Burroughs serve a less thematic end.

This purpose is related to Burroughs' strong convictions about the validity of the Darwinian theory of evolution. Porges documents this point in his biography.

An 1899 item, possibly of minor import, could, however, lead to some interesting speculation. The item, a book preserved throughout the years in Burroughs' personal library, is *Descent of Man*, by Charles Darwin (2nd Edition, Century Series, American Publishers Corporation, N.Y., 1874). On the flyleaf appears a notation "E. R. Burroughs Jan '99," and beneath it a pencil drawing by Ed of a large monkey or ape in a typical position, somewhat crouching, knuckles resting on the ground.

To Burroughs, Tarzan's development illustrated Darwin's ideas.[4]

During the Scopes trial in Tennessee, Burroughs wrote a strong defense of Darwinian evolution—and incidentally put to rest for all time the absurd idea that he was an atheist—in an article that appeared in the *New York American* for 6 July 1925.

It really does not make much difference what Mr. Scopes thinks about evolution, or what Mr. Bryan thinks about it. They cannot change it by thinking, or talking, or by doing anything else. It is an immutable law of Nature; and when we say that, it is just the same as saying that it is an immutable law of God—that is, for those who believe in God—for one cannot think of God and Nature as separate and distinct agencies.[5]

Throughout the novels, Burroughs not only makes references to the great apes as human and man-like, but also specifically describes them as representatives of an earlier stage of man's development, a kind of phylogenetic ancestor of modern man. The language is self-explanatory: "first men" (2.173), "forerunners of primitive man" (4.22), "fierce hairy progenitors of primitive man" (3.33), "great hairy primordial men" (4.90), and "primal seeds of humanity" (6.120).

Tarzan is the most famous fictional character who links man to his evolutionary past. The Greek and Roman heroes of ancient legend make concrete the transitional relationship between gods and men, for they show by personal example the origins of the hero as semi-divine; perhaps in analogous fashion, Tarzan stirs archetypal recollections of what we today believe to be our own origins. (Witness the absorbed fascination of the popular media with the work of the Leakeys and their successors at Olduvai.) There are many reasons for Tarzan's great popularity, but possibly this aspect of the character as the "missing link" is one of them. The Homeric world viewed the gods as its ancestors and deployed the hero as the visible proof for the possibility of such an origin; Burroughs' world conceives of the apes as man's ancestors, and the hero Tarzan becomes the embodiment of this idea.

At any rate it is clear what Burroughs has done with the starkly visible phenomenon of the gods in ancient literature. The concept of divinity would not work in Burroughs' universe, as it does in the ancient epics, but the obvious use Burroughs made of the concept, still present though in a different manifestation, may readily be seen as a remarkably fruitful and inventive adaptation of traditional material for new purposes. The hallmark of the writer who is knowledgeable in his tradition is his ability to profess openly his reliance on that tradition without giving in to a sterile copying of it. Our discussion has shown that Burroughs' apes owe an inestimable debt to the gods of classical literature, and, understood as a continuation of its divine machinery, their role in the heroic world of Tarzan may be properly assessed.

As we may speak of "minor" gods in Homeric and later Greek literature, so there are "minor" animals in the jungle of Tarzan who act in essentially supporting roles, some more prominently than others. The apes are the most important animals, especially in the first six novels, but they are by no means alone as nonhuman participants in the drama.

Some of these minor creatures serve the unidimensional end of food and are not extensively characterized. One never has a real sense of what they are like, as in the case of the apes. Bara the deer, for example, is a hapless victim of the Darwinian world in which Tarzan dwells, and we learn little about the animal. At the end of the first chapter of *Tales*, Tarzan mentions Bara among the animals who, unlike himself, have female companions and will have families. In other passages, Bara is a symbol of swiftness (1.67) or, as in *Jewels*, a hunted victim (5.105f.). It is invariably meek, fearful, defenseless, and gracefully lovely (6.64).

A similarly limited role is reserved to Horta the boar, who nevertheless has some breadth of character. We are told more about his appearance, and he is no timid victim like Bara. Horta is usually good for a fight (1.60). His features are given formulaic descriptions: his "short" (1.60) and "bristling neck" (1.68), the "formidable" (6.67) and "foam-flecked tusks" (1.68), and the "diabolical temper" (6.67).

Some of the animals are overtly hostile in their relationships to Tarzan. The crocodile, for example, is a formidable opponent (and a favorite, along with sharks and other reptiles, among the comic artists who draw Tarzan). No passage is more graphic than the lengthy one in *Beasts*, where the apeman is almost destroyed by a huge saurian. Caught in midstream (3.111), Tarzan is carried under water into the beast's lair and, though wounded, has succeeded in slaying the animal (3.116f.). This episode with the crocodile fulfills a typically retarding function within the larger narrative in which it stands, the vengeful hunting down of the villainous Rokoff. The animal is not described in any detail, but the contexts manage to evoke a satisfactory picture of slimy voraciousness.

The gorilla, who is quite distinct in Tarzan's jungle from the great anthropoid apes among whom he was reared, is an even more fearsome foe. Along with Tarzan we meet him for the first time early in *Tarzan*, where he is drawn in most horrid lines (1.144f.). He is a deadly enemy of the anthropoids and thus of Tarzan.

Dango the hyena, though usually a coward and reluctant to attack, can be emboldened by hunger (6.113). He is without exception an unpleasant animal, and he is quite fully characterized, especially in *Tales*, where the two hyenas of Bukawai the witch doctor attain almost symbolic status.

As a group, the carnivores are portrayed in most depth second only to the apes. With a few notable exceptions such as the panther in *Beasts* and Jad-bal-ja in *Tarzan and the Golden Lion*, the carnivores are a constant source of danger to Tarzan. Like minor malevolent spirits of the countryside, they stalk him relentlessly through the novels and, never successful in their attempt, are in turn stalked and taunted by him. The individual types within the group are lions, lionesses, leopards, and panthers, the last two being apparently indistinguishable, since both are called Sheeta. The typology of Numa the lion, almost as extensive as that of the apes, is characteristic of the group.

It would be unfair to suggest that these animals, destructive and cruel though they often prove, are incarnations of pure evil. With the possible exception of Histah the snake ("the most hated and loathed of all the jungle creatures"—6.61) or Dango the hyena, no animal is wholly "bad" in Tarzan's universe, and even Dango has his function as an eater of carrion. Man is the only beast who can be uncompromisingly evil in this universe.

Animals have an appointed place in the larger scheme, and though the relationship between Tarzan and the great cats is largely hostile, they have as much right to exist as any other animal, including man. There is no lord of creation. The view that Burroughs adopts for the animals in the jungle is essentially one of "ecological balance," a relationship that he imposed on his world long before it became the catchy slogan of the media. It is a basically unsentimental, straightforward notion of a natural harmony that is necessarily cruel in individual cases but functions remarkably well in the aggregate. Death is seen as part of life, and some animals must by nature kill in order to live. As the gods in ancient literature may be used to represent ideas and attitudes about what is right or wrong with human character and action, so the animals come to be used by Burroughs in a contrapuntal or antithetical technique for the development of his ideas about man's civilization and the way life is lived in it.

Animals in Burroughs, unlike the gods in Homer, are morally quite superior to the vast majority of human beings. To be a beast is not to be beastly or bestial, for beastness and bestiality or beastliness are two different categories. Neither quality readily implies the other, although both may be found in any one individual animal. Some beasts are bestial, but so are many humans; many beasts are also more humane than humans.

Tarzan feels himself to be very much part of the rhythms of nature and the unwritten laws by which the creatures of the jungle live. Since he is as much beast as he is man, he does not bring to the jungle that sullying and disturbing influence that man inevitably carries with him. For it is the "terrifying presence of man" (6.24) which brings grief to animals, and his is the "scent that sets the whole savage jungle aquiver" (2.190). Rarely if ever is the presence of man in the jungle beneficent, for he is an alien there (4.96); it usually entails exploitation or desecration of some sort. But this wanton and piggish destruction is of an entirely different order from the killing the animals (and Tarzan) practice on each other. The human intruders are motivated by greed and lust, but the animals and Tarzan by the need to survive. The animal and Tarzan wisely use the jungle, while the humans exploit it shamelessly.

Just as the Greek hero may be beset on all sides by hostile divinities as well as kindly ones, so Tarzan not only encounters the savage creatures who lurk in wait for him but also has a remarkable friendship with Tantor the elephant. Its very stability and endurance is perhaps best symbolized by the great bulk of the pachyderm. He balances, as it were, the many smaller but ill-willed animals who inhabit the jungle, and he offers a solid counterweight as helper and companion of Tarzan. In his relationship to Tarzan, he offers solace and quiet friendship; he listens attentively to Tarzan's musings, for he is a very "good listener" (6.184).

When Tarzan is in trouble, the loyal Tantor rescues him in great style (6.36). The sudden and unexpected epiphany of Tantor at 6.188 has overtones of the *deus ex machina*, the "god from the machine," made popular in Euripidean tragedy. An apparently hopeless situation with no conceivable solution is suddenly solved by the appearance of a rescuing "god" who simply sweeps the besieged human away from the messy complications of his life. Tantor, like one of these rescuing divinities, not only physicaly dispells the attackers, but also quite literally lifts Tarzan up on his back and lumbers off with him to the safety of Tarzan's cabin by the sea. It is very clear that if Tantor had not arrived when he did, Tarzan "would be a dead man" (6.187). A confrontation that might easily have resulted in a tragic outcome for the heroic protagonist is in the last moment transformed by the *animal ex machina*, as it were, and the novel ends on a witty and amusing note, Tarzan's rescue of the moon. This pattern of the near-disaster that is averted at the last moment for a favorable outcome is familiar enough from Greek tragedy (for example, Aeschylus' *Oresteia* and and Sophocles' *Philoctetes*). Like the other fauna, Tantor has a formulaic language similar to that of the apes and carnivores, but some of it understandably speaks to the unique physical characteristics of the giant.

In this connection, it may be pointed out that by language alone Burroughs has attempted to establish the fact of shared characteristics and, if not explicit, at least an implicit association among these animals. They hunt or are hunted, it is true, but they all belong to a huge cycle of existence from which no species is removable. The use of identical and similar language to describe quite different animals is perhaps a conscious reflection of the author's own preoccupation with the sense of unity and coherence that he wishes to impose on his world. The formulaic language becomes an almost subliminal tool for establishing identities and equalities among seemingly incommensurate characters.

By placing the apes and Tantor, as well as other animals, in a tradition to which the etymology of their generic and individual names points, Burroughs has underlined his own relationship to that earlier tradition. We know from Porges' biography that Burroughs kept meticulous files on the terminology he developed both for his Tarzan novels and for the Martian series,[6] and he made up names of the bizarre and strange characters and animals with which his prolific imagination populated also the desolate worlds of Barsoom. Porges comments at some length on Burroughs' peculiar adeptness for devising appropriate names for his people and animals. The classical tradition in which Burroughs had been so steeped in his younger years emerges with clarity: "On occasion he chose or modified words from foreign languages, *especially Latin.*[7] [Italics added]

Burroughs' abiding interest in the classical world is mirrored in the following citation of his *ipsissima verba* from a letter he wrote to his brother Harry on 2 July 1923.

I try to originate all the peculiar names for people, places and animals in my stories. Sometimes I must unconsciously use a word or name that I have read and forgotten, as for instance Numa the lion. There was a Roman emperor, Numa, of whom I had forgotten until I was recently rereading Plutarch's *Lives*. The name must have been retained in my sub-conscious brain, later popping out as original . . .[8]

Burroughs was, of course, wrong in calling Numa an emperor. Numa was a king (no small distinction in Roman history), but the point is self-evident. The essay to which Burroughs is referring must be the *Numa* or *Comparison of Lycurgus and Numa* by Plutarch; Numa was traditionally the successor of Romulus in the regal lists of Rome. His reign was a kind of golden age, and he himself was a great king. It is this regal quality or association in the name Numa that has transferred itself in Burroughs' mind to the lion, popularly known as the king of beasts.

The name for the hippopotamus, Duro, is suspiciously close to the Latin adjective *durus*, "harsh, rough, enduring," a not inappropriate appellation. The formation, then, is of a type commonly observed in the transition from Latin to modern Spanish, wherein Latin -*us* appears as -*o* in Spanish. (For example, Latin *caballus* goes to Spanish *caballo*, Latin *manus* to Spanish *mano*, and so forth.)

The buffalo is called Gorgo, which is simply the transliterated nominative Latin form of what has come into English as the bare stem, Gorgon. Ultimately, the word is Greek, Gorgo the female monster being etymologically very similar, if not related, to the Greek adjective *gorgos*, a word meaning "grim, fierce, terrible." There is something fierce about the jungle buffalo, although he is not quite the grim monster the Gorgon of ancient myth is.

It appears that the name of the boar, Horta, has been feminized from the masculine *hortus*, which is Latin for "garden." Despite the fact that the zebra is somewhat irascible and vicious, his name looks like an easy form from the Latin *paco*, "I make peaceful." Pisah the fish seems to carry at least remnants of his Indo-European heritage with him right into Tarzan's jungle, for the Indo-European root *PEISK appears in the familiar Latin word *piscis*, to which our own "fish" is in fact cognate.

Tantor, one feels, derives so much from the Latin adjective *tantus*, "so great," becoming a noun by the addition of the common Latin agent suffix -*or*. Tantor should, therefore, mean "he who is so great," which, one must admit, is not without merit as an apt name for the huge pachyderm.

The sun Kudu may conceivably derive its name from the Greek noun *kudos*, "glory," especially the kind of heroic glory whereof Homer speaks. And what is more glorious than the sun high in his heaven? The list could be expanded.

In concluding this discussion of Burroughs' obviously heavy and in part conscious indebtedness to classical Greek and Latin for these onomastic flights of fancy, we must look at the liquid name of his foster mother, Kala. The name is unmistakably Greek.[9] The extremely useful adjective *kalos* (masculine), *kale* or *kala* (feminine), and *kalon* (neuter) is one of the first words that the beginning student of classical Greek learns. One of the most common adjectives in ancient Greek, it speaks to those qualities of Greek culture which entail the concepts of the beautiful, the moral, the right, the fine, and so forth. Originally, it probably referred exclusively to external or physical beauty, but by the fifth century B.C. it had also come to refer to an interior beauty. The word has no single meaning, nor can it effectively be translated by any one English word. Whenever it appears in Greek it pushes out ripples of associations. That Burroughs the student of classical Greek just happened to call Tarzan's foster mother Kala, "she who is beautiful, good, fine," is hard to believe. To my knowledge Burroughs never explained why he chose this name for the great anthropoid, but there can be little doubt that he was reaching back into his first lessons in Greek and subsequent meetings with the word in Greek literature for the most perfect name imaginable. The nomenclature is imaginative, full of signification, and cleverly exploited; it is, we may say, the ultimate of connections between the world of classical antiquity and that of the great apes of Tarzan. The adjective itself, *kale*, of which *kala* is merely a dialect form, is used repeatedly in Homeric poetry of heroines and goddesses. The ape Kala has a glorious lineage!

Burroughs plays with the meaning of the word as a kind of calque of certain English adjectives. Consider some punning and verbal double-entendres of the sort he indulges in (italics added).

. . . for Kala was a *fine* clean -limbed young female . . . [1.53].
. . . while Kala *fairly* danced for joy and pride [1.62].
To Tarzan she had been kind, she had been *beautiful* [1.67].
She was a great, *fine* ape . . .[1.211].
. . . to me she was *beautiful* . . .[2.25].
of course Kala had been *beautiful* . . . (6.8).

But the ape and the notion of *kala* are more than these little word-plays. Throughout the corpus of the first six novels (and she is mentioned at least once in each novel, although she dies rather early in the first), Kala is spoken of in most favorable and commendatory terms. She is watchful of her charge, she educates him and brings him up in the right way, she shows extreme concern when he is hurt or wounded, she protects him in his infancy from the attacks of hostile members of the tribe, she loves and is loved in return—all her actions and all of Tarzan's memories of her after her death point to the very name she bears and epitomizes. She is fine and beautiful in every sense of the word, a kind of quintessential maternal femaleness.

The world of Tarzan, then, is as incomprehensible without the presence of all the animals in it as the world of Homer, of Greek tragedy, indeed of both Greek and Roman literature, is largely meaningless without the constant presence of the gods. Yet, it is inconceivable that the ancient readers of Ovid's *Metamorphoses*, for example, ever believed literally in those hundreds of deities and minor divinities who appear throughout the poem. They appreciated these gods, as did the audiences at Greek tragedy and Homeric recitations, as conventional devices that performed certain traditionally sanctioned functions in a literary context and had little, if anything, to do with the very different matter of a theological belief in gods.

Burroughs has taken over this divine machinery from the ancient tradition of heroic narratives, and the heroic figure of Tarzan, like the ancient hero with one foot in the world of gods and one in that of men, has been placed partially in the world of man and partially in the world of animals. So viewed, Tarzan is a truly traditional hero in the classical pattern, and, like the language and the technique discussed in earlier chapters, the animals as literary descendants of the ancient prototypes strongly underscore the heroic setting in which Tarzan exists.

It is to Tarzan himself, in his great complexity, that we now turn.

HERO

Tarzan is repeatedly said to have a dual nature, one human and one animal. His animal aspect gives him superhuman sensitivities of smell, hearing, and sight, as well as physical strength beyond the imagination of any mere man. But he also has intelligence of mind beyond that of any animal, and this mental acuity derives from generations of superb British stock. Like the best heroic types, Tarzan fits into a genealogy that has roots in human and nonhuman worlds. (See the chart in Appendix II for the particulars of his lineage.)

Since Tarzan kills his foster father Tublat at a relatively early stage, not much is made of Tublat as the "other" parent. It is the foster mother, Kala the she-ape, who is constantly held before the reader's eyes, even long after she has been killed by Kulonga the warrior (1.66f). The comparison between Lady Alice and Kala is one of the sustained synkrises of the novels, and it underscores the duality of Tarzan's origins.

From the many hundreds or even thousands of heroes in ancient literature and myth, it is not difficult to draw up an idealized schema of the heroic biography. No one hero may contain all the items in the pattern, but a sufficient number apply so that a character does fit or does not fit into a lengthy and well-developed tradition. Such generalized guides have been constructed from the known lives of heroes, and one of the fuller and more useful examples is that done by Lord Raglan[1] (see Appendix III).

In the following analysis of Tarzan's congruence with the paradigm of the heroic type, no suggestion is made that Burroughs sat down and drew up a similar pattern. It would not be surprising, however, if he had done just that, for we know that from his earliest years he was fascinated by classical myth and culture. A letter dated 13 February 1887 from his older brother George, written to Burroughs in reply to one from him, underscores the point. Burroughs himself specifically credited his fascination with the ancient Roman legend about the suckling of Romulus and Remus by a she-wolf for the origin of Tarzan, himself suckled by a she-ape.[2]

The profusion of heroic motifs and the displacements they have undergone in Burroughs' hero are indicative of a composite and eclectically conceived protagonist. He may well be Romulus (or Remus), but he is also Heracles, Achilles, Odysseus, Perseus, Telemachus, Orestes, and countless other specific heroes. It is not strange that Burroughs, who had read widely in the classics and who, by his own admission, was inordinately fond of classical mythology, should have come up with a hero as classical, even in smaller details, as Tarzan. Consciously or not, Burroughs created his Tarzan in the classical mold.

We should expect Tarzan's *vita* to conform to a reasonable number of the categories suggested by Lord Raglan. The first category indicates that the hero's mother is a royal virgin, but it is simply not true of Tarzan's mother. What we do find, however, is a displaced form of this element in that Tarzan's mother, Alice Clayton, was not only a member of the peerage by marriage, as Lady Greystoke (1.4), but was also in her own right of the nobility, as is clear from her maiden title, the Honorable Alice Rutherford (1.2). Tarzan's father, though not a king (the second category), is described as "a certain young English nobleman," and he was not without "political ambition" (1.2), both points which may be construed as vestigial of a regal prototype. Clearly it is impossible to entertain a reasonable suspense of disbelief in the trekking of a king and his queen alone into Africa in the late 1880s. Therefore, the necessary toning down of this part of Tarzan's biography has been dictated by the exigencies of the hero's placement in a modern world.

The third category, the relationship of the mother to the father, is completely missing in Burroughs. As for the fourth category, it is not so much the circumstances of Tarzan's conception but those of his birth that are so peculiar. For although his conception in England can only have been normal, no one would deny that the circumstances of his birth in Africa were extremely unusual.

Let us take the next category (5). Although Tarzan is often called god-like, except by certain natives he is never reputed to be divine or the son of a god. We have seen in the previous chapter what the "gods" have become in Burroughs, and Tarzan is, of course, thought to be the son of the apes. But it would transcend any fictional license to suggest that the human Tarzan was born of two apes or that he sprang from an ape's union with a human. A fictionally credible accommodation has to be made, which is simply that he has dual parentage. It is this alleged nonhuman heritage which links him to the heroic type, since the latter has a "god" (Burroughs' apes) somewhere in the immediate genealogy. It is in this connection that the next three categories (6, 7, and 8) may best be discussed.

No attempt is made on Tarzan's life at the moment of his birth, but in the narrative we are immediately transported forward one year in time, for a "year from the day her little son was born Lady Alice passed quietly away in the night" (1.25). It is at this point that the great apes of the tribe of Kerchak make their appearance in the cabin.

When the king ape released the limp form which had been John Clayton, Lord Greystoke, he turned his attention toward the little cradle; but Kala was there before him, and when he would have grasped the child she snatched it herself, and before he could intercept her she had bolted through the door and taken refuge in a high tree [1.30].

The attempt on Tarzan's life is unsuccessful, and although some of the apes object to Kala's new infant, she is allowed to keep him as though he were her own. Tarzan is not exactly "spirited away" (category 7), since he is already in a far country, but he is certainly being raised by foster parents (category 8). More to the point is that Tarzan, when he is removed from the crib in his parents' cabin, is metaphorically whisked out of one world into a completely novel one. The distance of removal may not be large in geographical terms, but it is nonetheless immense.

Category 9 is valid for Tarzan but requires some qualification. We have just seen how uneventful the apeman's first year of life was; the next few years are passed over with equal rapidity, and we pick up on him as a character at age ten (1.35), when his "activity" proper commences. In the next twenty-five pages or so (1.35–63), we move along with Tarzan through the compressed account of his prodigious feats of self-education in both the physical and mental spheres.

When Tarzan is eighteen (1.64) his activity, as that term is understood in relation to the hero, truly begins. He meets man for the first time in the form of Kulonga, who slays Kala. The rest of the book only brings us to Tarzan's very early twenties and is devoted to the larger subject of Tarzan's (re-) discovery of love and civilization.

In connection with category 10, it is difficult to determine which is Tarzan's real "kingdom," for he is inherently a straddler of two worlds. He has property in England, but also "vast estates in Uziri" (3.7). In fact, Tarzan establishes himself in both kingdoms. After the death of his cousin, William Cecil Clayton (2.216), Tarzan comes into his rightful inheritance as the true Lord Greystoke, and the jungle he already has as his kingdom. How did he come to be a king (categories 11–13)?

Raised among the apes of the tribe of Kerchak, Tarzan at one point came into conflict with the king. No great love had ever existed between Kerchak and Tarzan, and in the apeman's infancy only Kala's vigilance prevented Kerchak (or some other ape) from destroying him. When Kala does die, Tarzan is old enough to take care of himself, and shortly after her death the confrontation with Kerchak occurs. The old king suddenly goes berserk and lashes out at any unfortunate ape in his way. He challenges his hated adversary to combat, and after a redoubtable contest Tarzan emerges the winner —his unknown father's knife gave him the victory over the huge Kerchak and made him a king (1.97).

Although Tarzan enters civilization and travels to Europe and America at the end of Tarzan, the adjustment is not a happy one, nor, in Return, when he is forced by external circumstances back to the very jungle from which he had set out (1.96), is he chagrined. Even after many years of civilized life in England, Tarzan is still quite ambivalent about his true preferences, for he is torn between the claims of his English heritage and its many family obligations, and of the upbringing and life he had lived in the jungle. Hence, there is no question that Tarzan is on a journey to and from his various king-doms, but it is unfair to call either the future kingdom to the exclusion of the other, for both are future kingdoms simultaneously, and Tarzan's constant movement between the two serves to underscore the ineradicable duality of his nature.

Coming back to category 11, we must make some qualifications. While Tarzan was victorious over Kerchak, Tarzan's life has long been one of mortal battles with "a giant, dragon or wild beast." Bolgani the gorilla was the first victim of Tarzan's intelligence and his father's knife, and many lions, leopards, deer, and other animals gave him subsequent victories. These beasts of the jungle have their more terrifying analogues in the bestial monsters that stalk about in civilization, and we may note that even these human antagonists fall into the general pattern of monsters and harmful creatures whose pernicious influence the hero, in his wandering, must remove from the earth.

The individualized pattern of destruction of the king begins with the removal of Kerchak, but it is by no means restricted to that incident. In many situations in the novels, Tarzan (or, in *Son*, Korak) must once more remove a king or leader in order to make his own authority preeminent (for example, 1.92, 2.149, 3.23, 3.26, 4.90, and 6.187). It is a sophisticated technique of introducing narrative varia-tion into the rather pedestrian device of repetition. How, in other words, can the reader fail to appreciate the heroic leadership of Tarzan after having been reminded of his "accesssion" on so many occasions?

Moving on to the conclusion of Raglan's pattern, we note from the chapter following Tarzan's killing of Kerchak that Tarzan does indeed become a lawgiver of sorts and that this life assumes a rather uneventful direction. His leadership is good for the apes, for his greater intelligence can both conceive and execute plans that are conducive to the betterment of their life. His tug in the direction of human concerns, however, causes prolonged absences from the tribe, and these absences are keenly felt among the apes, to such a degree that he is reprimanded by some of them (1.90). There follows a humorous account of the petty squabbles and frivolous contretemps that occur in the diurnal existence of apes and that must be adjudicated by Tarzan lest they develop into forces disruptive of the whole society.

In a somewhat similar fashion, Tarzan assumes control over the battle strategy of the Waziri, lays down the conditions for success against the enemy, and is able to bring off a victory.

This analysis takes us through category 15 in Raglan's list, and all but no. 3 (the father and mother are close relatives) and no. 12 (marriage to a princess) are present. Beyond reasonable question, Tarzan does fit the heroic pattern as outlined by Raglan, a pattern that could be duplicated from other sources without substantive changes in the gross outlines. In the final categories (16–22), however, the fit is perhaps more equivocal. Tarzan does not die in the first six books (or later, for that matter), nor does he as a result become the object of formal cult worship as a hero. Burroughs has nevertheless made certain accommodations in an ideal pattern of the heroic *vita* that permit us to discern some of these categories in Tarzan's biography, albeit in faded or displaced configurations.

Tarzan never quite loses favor with the "gods" (apes and animals) in such a way that he is driven from the throne. Indeed, his "people" prosper under his guidance in ways that they never had under Kerchak (1.88). It is rather a question of the "people" or "gods" losing favor with Tarzan so that it is he who desires to leave them (1.91). The thematic element is the same, but the roles have been inverted.

There are also those incidents, such as at the end of *Tales*, in which the apes threaten to kill Tarzan because he is too different from themselves. Although he is not killed, the intent is there, and the point about his many differences from the apes and from the community in which he lives does address itself to the typical apartness of the classical hero. Achilles in Homer, like Ajax in Sophocles or Hippolytus in Euripides or Daphnis in Theocritus or countless other heroic types in other authors, does not fit or cannot fit himself into the larger society in which he has been raised and lives. Apartness proves to be one feature of the hero that distinguishes him from the general population of his age. Thus, the attempts on Tarzan's life may be seen as a "faded" form of death.

Many heroes (Odysseus, Heracles, and Aeneas, to name a few) do at some point in their career make a *katabasis* (journey down) into the lower world, a descent into Hell, as part of a symbolic death before rebirth and return as a renewed and wiser hero. Prototypical of the heroic *katabasis* is the journey to a distant land, often one that lies far beyond the known world or that is only tangentially connected to it. The entrance itself is usually a grove or cave or similar opening into the earth whereby access is to be gained into Hell itself; the place is invariably murky or dark. The earliest description of this theme in Western literature, in Book 11 of Homer's *Odyssey*, also happens to be one of the fullest.

This thematic element in the heroic life is handled grandly in *Jewels*. Opar is a "lost" civilization in the midst of Africa, tracing its ancestry back to the legendary Atlantis, and it is in Opar that Tarzan is temporarily "killed." Just as the land of the Kimmerians and Ocean, a huge girdling river about the earth, is outside the "real" world of Odysseus, so the land of Opar is a "weird, dead city of the long-dead past" in which "it seemed that there should be no life, for living things seemed out of place" (2.162). And Opar is as hard of access and as removed from the world as any classical Hell (2.160).

The descent into the valley where Opar is situated is described in terms not wholly unlike those which Vergil used in his *Aeneid* for Aeneas' descent into the lower world. First, Burroughs:

There was no trail, but the way was less arduous than the ascent of the opposite face of the mountain had been. Once in the valley, their progress was rapid. . . [2.161].

Next, Vergil:

. . . the trip down to Avernus is easy (the door of dark Wealth stands open day and night), but to retrace one's steps and get up into the air above —there is the task, there is the toil! [*Aeneid* 6.126–129].

Tarzan enters the inner precincts of Opar alone (2.164). This full rehearsal of Opar in *Return* is largely repeated in *Jewels*. The city is once more "frightful" (5.13) and "dead" (5.14), and it is located in a "desolate valley" (5.31, 5.44). Although the Waziri accompany Tarzan on this expedition into Opar, they do not follow him into the treasure vault but leave before he does and are not caught by the earthquake that buries Tarzan inside the massive fortifications of the ancient city. Tarzan does not die, of course, but there is more than a vestige of this thematic category in the viewpoint which the author assigns to the Waziri who come in search of Tarzan (5.31). Furthermore, the fact that the apeman is trapped in an underground chamber that happens also to be a treasure vault is not without bearing on the reading of this episode as Tarzan's "death." The lower world in classical myth is typically a place of immense wealth and kingly treasure, ruled by Hades, and aside from the magnificent dwellings which he occupies, it is a place of gloom. The physical appearance of Opar itself is one that sparkles and scintillates. Tarzan approaches the "golden domes and minarets of Opar" in the dark of the night (5.22). Indeed, the language is reminiscent of Aeneas' famous start for the lower world.

Ibant obscuri sola sub nocte per umbram (Beneath the lonely night they started out dimly through the shadow . . .)[*Aeneid* 6.268].

And in Burroughs:

With the coming of night he set forth . . . . [5.22].

It is, therefore, reasonable to allow a conditional inclusion of category 18 from Raglan's list. Tarzan does not die in the way that Heracles, for example, dies, but he does perish after the fashion of those heroes who die to the world when they leave it for adventure or information in Hell. Tarzan's "return to life" occurs late in the book (5.143) after Burroughs has led his hero on a lengthy quest for his own identity, for, like the classical heroes who make the journey into Hades' house, Tarzan, too, learns something about who he is.

The last four categories cannot be found in any guise in the six novels. Nor, since Tarzan does not physically die, should this lack be striking. Raglan's list here indicates a common phenomenon in the ancient world, namely, the tendency to make an important individual within a community or family into something of a cult figure or object of worship after his death. It has no application for Burroughs' adaptation of the heroic cycle to his protagonist. It is clear, however, that the very conception of Tarzan is deeply rooted in the heroic literature of classical Greece and Rome. Equally evident by now is the careful allegiance which, in his creation of Tarzan, Burroughs has shown to the many nameless exemplars that have coalesced into his hero from his own reading. Burroughs himself was willing enough to concede that "such a story might have been written fifteen years ago or fifteen hundred years ago: '. . . there is nothing new in the idea nor have I claimed there was anything new in it. It has been used repeatedly from the time of Romulus and Remus and probably long before.'"³ Tarzan must be understood as a completely and thoroughly traditional hero with an inalienable place in the upper branches of that literary tree whose roots are deeply embedded in the still fertile soil of the Greek and Roman classics.

Let us take the hero Odysseus as a basic analogy for our discussion of the huge body of material that presents Tarzan to the reader. Great amounts of formulaic vocabulary cluster around Odysseus, and from the individual epithets in the *Odyssey* we obtain a rather detailed description. One aspect of this is his genealogy, which accounts for the common patronymic formula "son of Laertes." Further definition is seen in the toponymic epithet "Ithacan" or "the man from Ithaca." The hero's remoter origin from the gods is constantly held before the audience in such epithets as "divine," "god-like," "godly," and "god-born." His reputation precedes him in the frequent epithets "noble," "glorious," "blameless," "magnanimous" and "famous." Since Odysseus is a hero whose strengths are more mental or spiritual than physical, most of the epithets that speak to his characteristic nature deal with mental attributes. But he is also a man of action, and the common "city-sacker" explains itself. In the later tradition, however, as well as in Homer himself, the qualities for which Odysseus is legendary are his cunning endurance and mental alertness. A number of epithets appear frequently to highlight this facet of his personality. He is "much-minded," "much-planning," "much-devising," "much-enduring," "shifty-wiled," "stout-minded," and "shrewd."

Theses epithets are not applied to Odysseus alone, but, as was the case with the attributives of deities, they move freely among different men and even between the worlds of men and gods. It is important to realize that the epithets, whatever their historical origins may have been, function as unifiers of the two worlds in much the same way that unrestrained movement of epithets from animals to Tarzan unites the two groups and emphasizes their close interrelation.

Among the many epithets applied to Tarzan that recur with great frequency are "lithe," "bronzed," "smooth," "brown," and "muscular."

Tarzan is not, however, a muscleman. Indeed, Burroughs was not happy with the first movie-Tarzan, Elmo Lincoln, who played in *Tarzan of the Apes*, because he was "far from my conception of the character. . . . Tarzan was not beefy but was light and graceful and well muscled. . . . Then he must be the epitome of grace. . . . My conception of him is a man a little over six feet tall and built more like a panther than an elephant. . . ."[4] And so we find liberal use of such adjectives as "supple" and "graceful." Burroughs admitted that he "was rather prone to use superlatives,"[5] and he does not hesitate, in spite of his formulations regarding the ideal Tarzan, to call him "giant" on many occasions, as well as "tall," "big," "huge," and "great." The first impression that Tarzan gives is of a "superb physique" (1.214).

As might be expected, the musculature of the apeman is presented in a highly formulaic vocabulary, among which are such terms as "giant," "mighty," "steel," "massive," "rolling," "like Numa's," and "immense." The best concise characterization of the physical appearance of the apeman is given in *Tarzan*, which serve as a summary of the above details.

His straight and perfect figure, muscled as the best of the ancient Roman gladiators must have been muscled, and yet with the soft and sinuous curves of a Greek god, told at a glance the wondrous combination of enormous strength with suppleness and speed [1.97].

Here one notes the merging, even if stereotyped, of the two cultures in Burroughs' classical hero, the might of Rome and the beauty of Greece.

At the same time that the novels are filled with these generalized accounts of Tarzan's appearance, great pains are taken with the description of individual details. Of the many features that are described over and over again with a comforting regularity, few are as persistently held before us as Tarzan's eyes. The impression is that Burroughs believed the eyes to be the mirror of the man, for the epithets he applies to them cover a staggering range of possibilities. Tarzan's eyes are rather consistently characterized as "intelligent," "jungle-trained," "laughing," "keen," "sharp," "frank," "alert," "bright," and "quick." These epithets are obviously more descriptive of Tarzan than of his eyes, and they become vehicles for extended characterization of the apeman himself. In addition to these laudatory descriptions of Tarzan and his eyes, less favorable terms come into play. His eyes can also be "savage" and "fierce" when they reflect his anger and are "blazing with the passion of hate and vengeance" (3.81) or display a "savage glint" (5.90). Such a "nasty light" (2.48) recalls the formula used of Achilles when he is upset or angry, *hypodra idon*, a phrase that means something like "with an under(handed) look," "with a grim look."

But by far the most persistent epithet of Tarzan's eyes is the one that describes their color, grey. Indeed, when Tarzan is angry, the grey color becomes a "cold, grey" (2.32) or "steel-gray" (2.29). Curiously, Burroughs (or the printers) are inconsistent in the spelling of the color, for it appears variously as "grey" (for example, 3.80) and "gray" (for example, 2.17). Perhaps the prominence of this epithet is felt so strongly because it also lurks in the titular name *Grey*stoke, which may simply point to a genetic fact about the line from which Tarzan comes and which he perpetuates. At any rate, we are explicitly told that the eyes of Tarzan's father were grey (1.2), and his sons eyes are likewise grey (4.20).

There is no need to give all of the repetitive epithets employed in defining the parts of Tarzan's body, but as formulaic as the description of the eyes is, in general, that of the face, head, limbs, torso, and extremities. The highly stylized language that defines the physical Tarzan points up the typically repetitious way in which the hero is depicted. It is the same type of repetition that is so well developed in the Homeric descriptions of heroes, although Burroughs is more specific in his delineations. In much the same way, then, that Homer presented his heroes to his audience, Burroughs, whether consciously or not, is presenting his hero to the reader through constant repetition. The hero gains definition from the conventional vocabulary, and at the same time the vocabulary itself verges on the proprietary.

Epithets and phrases are far more important as indicators of Tarzan's personality than of the anatomy itself. Their use is well established in the tradition, but Burroughs has developed them further than Homer. Burroughs presses them into service as very convenient and almost subliminal cues in the general characterization of the hero, which is thus accomplished with great economy. When judgmental adjectives are brought into play in the description of the physical man, his emotional and psychological personality is being put before the reader's inspection. It is a procedure both satisfying and in accord with tradition to describe the hero—who traditionally has both a physical and a mental or spiritual component to this makeup—in such a way that the characterization of his physical nature is made also to comment on the more internal aspects of his being.

When with "nimble fingers" (6.22) Tarzan unties the thongs that keep Taug imprisoned, we do not learn as much about his motivation or emotional commitment as when we read in the previous paragraph that Tarzan with "relentless fingers" (6.22) choked to death the guard on duty before Taug's cage. The former epithet describes a facile dexterity that in no real sense gives us an insight into Tarzan's character. The latter epithet, however, probes beneath the surface of those fingers and suggests something about the mind and heart that direct their action. In similar fashion, that a "great hand" (2.41) is clamped about an enemy's windpipe is not greatly illuminating of Tarzan the killer, but when we are told that "awful fingers" (2.141) were doing the job, we are also being informed about the quality of the action and the nature of the doer. Again, when it is the "steel fingers" (6.163) of Tarzan which are choking the life out of the witch doctor, we do not become as deeply engaged in the action as when we read that "cruel fingers" (6.165) are on the man's throat.

It is precisely this matter of engaging the reader and, if even at a barely conscious level, forcing him to react in some way to the evaluative epithets that is important: was Tarzan justified? did the victim deserve his fate? where do our sympathies lie? how does the author wish us to react? We perhaps do not even realize it, but after slipping in a few such epithets, Burroughs has quietly coerced the reader into building up an image of the character and adopting an attitude towards him and his actions. Characterization by such indirection is not new with Burroughs but has solid antecedents in the heroic literature of antiquity. Although Homer was not overly given to define or evaluate characters and events by this means, the Roman poet Vergil developed it into high art in his *Aeneid*.[6]

Much is made of Tarzan's voice and the staggering range of

sounds it can produce. This aspect of his being assumes a fairly prominent position in the general prosopography of the apeman. The strongly formulaic language that is used in this connection once more points up Tarzan's ambivalent nature, for it defines him on the one hand as human and on the other, and more commonly, as a beast. His voice becomes, in effect, another vehicle for examining the complex origin and development of the protagonist. Just as Tarzan's voice turns into a means for auctorial comment on the persona of the protagonist, so his smile fulfills much the same function. It is frequently referred to in the novels and takes on both epithets and psychological coloring in the ongoing delineation of the apeman. A favored epithet is "grim" (as at 2.13, 3.36, 4.212). Death, whether his own or another's, is at times an occasion for Tarzan's amusement, and "when Tarzan killed he more often smiled than scowled" (1.162).

His smile is not exclusively an indicator of the lust for battle, however; it may also reveal genuine humor. After he has played a practical joke on the apes with whom he lives, Tarzan gets a rise out of them, much to his own vast amusement (6.125). The quality of kindness that Tarzan possesses reveals itself in a smile on his face, meant to reassure the young Arab woman terrified by Tarzan's victory cry over a slain lion (2.90). Every grim smile of disapproval is balanced by the smile of approval on Tarzan's face when he sees how effectively Meriem is able to deal with the savage dogs kept in his compound (4.117). This minor detail of his smile, like that of Tarzan's voice and other physical aspects, can also prove to be indicative of the inner man and his attitudes.

A final point remains to be treated in connection with the physical Tarzan: his motion. We know that Tarzan is fast (1.51), nimble (5.73), and agile (3.125), and it is worthwhile to consider the explicit and implicit comparisons that are drawn between Tarzan and animals in this respect. The analogy is quite natural insofar as Tarzan lives among these beasts to whom he is compared, but one should not at the same time ignore the great frequency with which Homeric heroes are explicitly likened to various animals in the longish similes that more closely define them, their actions, and motivations.

Tarzan is admittedly "swifter than his heavy fellows" (6.61), the apes, but a more accurate impression of his speed comes from the many comparisons to those who are not his fellows in the jungle. Often it is the enemies who figure in the analogies, as in a scene in *Tales*. The passage in question (6.58) is very Homeric in other respects besides the likeness of Tarzan to a lion. Tarzan has entered the village of Mbonga and knows that he is being followed by the chief, when the following action is played out.

When Mbonga, therefore, came within spear range of the apeman, the latter suddenly wheeled upon him, so suddenly that the poised spear was shot a fraction of a second before Mbonga had intended. It went a trifle high and Tarzan stooped to let it pass over his head; then he sprang toward the chief. But Mbonga did not wait to receive him. Instead, he turned and fled for the dark doorway of the nearest hut, calling as he went for his warriors to fall upon the stranger and slay him.

   Well indeed might Mbonga scream for help, for Tarzan, young and fleet-footed, covered the distance between them in great leaps, at the speed of a charging lion [6.58].

Not only does this passage evoke the speed of the lion as applicable to Tarzan, but also, by substituting the names of Mbonga and Tarzan for those of the Trojan Hector and Greek Achilles, respectively, we might be reading one of the formulaic battle sequences in the *Iliad*. The epithet applied to Tarzan here is perhaps not fortuitous, as "fleet-footed" (or, as the Greek *podas okus* is usually rendered, "swift-footed") is a traditional epithet for Achilles. The idea of a warrior hurling his spear and missing his target or hitting it without effect is a virtual cliché of the Homeric battle scene, as Bernard Fenik has illustrated at great length in his important monograph.[7] Nor is it unusual in the Homeric combats to find one of the contestants making a hurried exit from the battle, much as Mbonga does, in spite of having set himself up as something of a terror (cf. *Iliad* 3.30ff.). Finally, Tarzan's attack "at the speed of a charging lion" is familiar to the readers of Homer, where not only Achilles but also many other heroes are from time to time likened to a lion. Thus, in Book 20 of the *Iliad* when Achilles is about to engage the Trojan warrior Aeneas, he is said to have "rushed like a lion, destructive" against Aeneas (20.164f.). The strongly Homeric tone of the passage in *Tales* is undeniable.

   In the novels, Burroughs develops an elaborate and highly formulaic vocabulary for describing Tarzan's actual movements in transporting himself from one place to another. In ancient literature, there is, of course, a set of formulas that "move" characters about, such as "they went off" (*ban d'imenai* at *Iliad* 20.32), "they went in a line" (*estichon* at 16.258), and "he rushed" (*orto* at 5.590). The variety of the phrases as well as the different types of action to which they refer give to the *Iliad* its sense of commotion and at times frantic movement.

The impression of constant action in Burroughs' novels is created in no small degree by the formulas of verbs and phrases that describe Tarzan's movements. Since motion is such an integral part of Tarzan's character, it is also one of the strong recommendations for Burne Hogarth that he alone of the illustrators seems to have understood and exploited this feature of Tarzan, just as he has obviously recognized the importance of Burroughs' psychological jungle and reflected this recognition in his superb delineations of the jungle backgrounds. Hogarth, perhaps the greatest of the many illustrators who have done Tarzan comics, newspaper strips, and books, makes highly imaginative use of space in the single panel and in the layout of the several panels on the page so that one does get that same unmistakable sense of urgency, vibrant and controlled movement, and aliveness. Hogarth's is the perfect visualization of Burroughs' verbal image.

The type of verbal convention that is under discussion here is not by any means to be construed as indicative of careless or unimaginative writing, any more than the Homeric repetitions are. Rather it suggests both narrative economy and a strong auctorial sense for the characterization of the hero. The hero is the one stable and predictable character in the hostile jungle world, and by repeated confirmation of an unchanging core the author fashions a hero of strength, durability, and constancy. Since the Homeric tone of such formulaic conventions is absolutely unmistakable, the hero so described takes on the equally unmistakable aura of the heroic type. Like the language, he endures.

But true depth is given the character of the physical Tarzan by elaboration of his mental and spiritual qualities. He is anything but the simple-minded cretin that television and film have made him out to be in the nonreading imagination. A favorite epithet for Tarzan's brain is "active." In contrast to the apes among whom he has grown up, Tarzan dreamed dreams and had an understanding unknown to them because of his "active brain" (1.91). As Burroughs states elsewhere, Tarzan was "active in brain as he was in body" (6.106). The productivity of his mental life is pointed out in the attribute "fertile," as in the "fertile brain" (6.8) that devises jungle games for Tarzan and his playmates. It is this "fertile manmind" (6.37), "clever" (1.40), "alert" (6.21), and "inquisitive" (6.179), which helps Tarzan to attain his indisputable supremacy over the beasts of the forest who are much more powerful physically than he is. The brain is the key The quality of the intelligence that resides in Tarzan's mind is, as we might well expect, of a "high order" (6.152) and "superior" (1.39) to that of the apes. Examples of his powers of mind abound throughout the novels, and both his inventiveness and curiosity speak to some degree to that part of his literary origin that is the Trickster. This important aspect of the characterization of Tarzan will be discussed in detail on pages 120-129.

Tarzan's curiosity is evident from early in his childhood, especially concerning the cabin his father built (for example, 1.41, 1.47, and 6.48). Closely related to his curiosity about the world is his inventiveness, which manifests itself in diverse ways. We are first made aware of this index to his intelligence in the passage in *Tarzan* where he exploits the properties of the rope that he has devised for himself by "twisting and tying long grasses together" (1.39). One day in play he happens to discover that a rope can be used as a lasso. He transforms his erstwhile toy into a potent weapon, the first unhappy object of which is Tarzan's hated stepfather, the ape Tublat. Alert as the apeboy is to the possibilities inherent in any novel situation, Tarzan also discovers the principle of momentum that enables him to use a rope as a swing (6.106); he has devised a crude razor blade to shave his face and trim his hair (6.160); and, in general, he has eliminated boredom from his life by varying the stern demands of his dangerous existence with "activities of his own invention" (6.159).

An unintelligent creature fails to realize when it has hit upon something useful or when a particularized action can be generalized for different circumstances. Tarzan, however, picks up on these unexpected bits of experience in such a way that they become incorporated into the general pattern of his life. His knife, for example (itself symbolic of Tarzan's heritage left him by his English father), is perhaps the central tool in his rather extensive armamentarium. It comes to occupy that position because Tarzan's mind was able to generalize about its effect from the particular incident when he fought huge Bolgani the gorilla and inadvertently killed him (1.44). This is not to say that Tarzan is an intellectual. He clearly is not. But he is highly intelligent and evidently sees nothing wrong with the pursuit of intellectual and, one might say, academic interests. Certainly the whole narrative about his learning to read underscores not only the eagerness with which he embarked on the acquisition of knowledge but also the great delight and joy he found in giving himself over to these diversions.

Tarzan's genuine devotion to matters of the mind and his development of aesthetic sensibilities are apparent long before he meets any human beings. Burroughs handles the entire episode in *Tales* that deals with Tarzan's discovery of the sense of deity with a certain pantheistic profundity. He gives the reader a very clear view of the hero as an individual grappling with some of the "higher" concerns of human existence. Tarzan's simultaneous awareness of the existence of beauty as a thing delightful and worthwhile in its own right indicates that he is obtuse in neither the aesthetic nor the teleological sphere (6.48–64, the chapter entitled "The God of Tarzan").

With age and exposure to Western civilizations, Tarzan is in a position to cultivate these apparently innate tendencies. When he lives in Paris after his unsuccessful suit of Jane Porter, the intellectually curious apeman takes full and enthusiastic advantage of the cultural offerings the capital can afford him in its great museums and magnificent libraries. Despite his basically nonintellectual character, Tarzan does display one fatal illusion in which so many intellectual types indulge, especially during their younger years (Tarzan is twenty-two years old at this point—see 2.9). He bemoans the hopelessness of mastering even the smallest portion of the totality of human knowledge and artistic achievement.

Tarzan spent the two following weeks renewing his former brief acquaintance with Paris. In the daytime he haunted the libraries and picture galleries. He had become an omnivorous reader, and the world of possibilities that were opened to him in this seat of culture and learning fairly appalled him when he contemplated the very infinitesimal crumb of the sum total of human knowledge that a single individual might hope to acquire even after a lifetime of study and research [2.25f.].

Part of Tarzan's overwhelming appeal as a protagonist is precisely his boundless potential to become anything he wants to be. He combines the best of the man who is physically active and intellectually inquisitive, and both possibilities are part of his British aristocratic roots. Tarzan is able to bridge the two worlds of knowledge and action, for in understanding the one in terms of the other, he has unified these two primary areas of human experience, word and deed, thought and action, mind and body.

Reason it is which makes Tarzan speculate about the universe and the things that are in it, and by a type of deductive analogy he devises a reasoned explanation for the existence of the moon and stars. This cosmogonic etiology is based on empirical evidence. (Tarzan is, after all, British, and not in the Germanic metaphysical tradition.) He has just observed that a party of natives caught in the jungle for the duration of the night built a fire in order to ward off the prowling cats and other animals bent on attack, and he transforms this experience into an account for the existence of the black sky with its many "eyes" and one shining face (of Goro the moon) (6.181). We may smile at Tarzan's explanation, but an earlier, mythopoeic age would surely have concurred in his account.

Tarzan also comes to grips with the ancient philosophical dichotomy between illusion and reality. In his own way, he is forced into a confrontation with pure abstractions like "the real" and "the illusory." In one of the more intellectually appealing passages in Burroughs, the hero, generally but erroneously typed as all muscle and action, exhibits precisely those mental activities which place him far above the level of the animals in his world. The circumstances are the following. The natives of Mbonga's village are feasting on the cooked flesh of Tantor the elephant, and Tarzan filches some meat from one of their cooking pots. Without knowing that the animal had died of disease, he eats it but does not like the taste. He falls into an uncomfortable and fitful sleep. When he wakes up it is daylight, and a lion is chasing him; greatly to

Tarzan's surprise, the animal begins to climb the tree in which he has been sleeping (6.132). Tarzan is unable to outclimb his pursuer, for the lion goes as high in the branches as he. When the lion has followed him out to the tip of the topmost and slenderest branches, it appears that the end has come. Suddenly, a monstrous bird descends on Tarzan and plucks him up in its huge talons to whisk him away from the claws of the lion. As the bird flies higher and higher, the jungle grows dim and the sun hotter, until Tarzan "comes to his senses" and begins to fight back by attacking the bird with his hunting knife. The talons of the bird relax their grip, and Tarzan falls to the ground for several minutes, hitting the branch he had been sleeping on. He topples, but just in time catches himself and avoids a fall. He is amazed to find that it is suddenly night again.

The entire experience leaves Tarzan confused, and his attempt to explain what has happened takes on strongly Platonic overtones.

He could not believe what he had seen and yet, having seen these incredible things, he could not disbelieve the evidence of his own perceptions. Never in all his life had Tarzan's senses deceived him badly, and so, naturally, he had great faith in them. Each perception which ever had been transmitted to Tarzan's brain had been, with varying accuracy, a true perception. [6.134].

Still marveling at this categorical repudiation of what he knows to be the truth and the natural order of things, he is once more dumbfounded by the sudden appearance of a huge snake wearing the face of the native he had killed in order to procure the meat. When he strikes at this monster, it disappears; now awake, he looks around to see what happened to it. Many dreams interspersed with moments of awakening fill the remainder of his night, and the next day he makes his way to his father's cabin. There he finds a picture of the bird that had carried him away during the night. He also looks at a story about Bolgani the gorilla, and exhausted from the previous night, he dozes off while reading. At this point, the cabin door opens and Bolgani the gorilla enters. Tarzan sees immediately that Bolgani is "in the throes of that jungle madness that seizes upon so many of the fiercer males" (6.138). Tarzan reaches for his knife on the table and at the same time catches sight of the pictures of Bolgani in the book he has been reading; he will not be fooled again (6.139). Amazingly, however, the gorilla does not change in the expected ways. Rather, it attacks Tarzan and starts to carry him off. In alarm, Tarzan tries to get away, and the animal "buried great fangs in a sleek, brown shoulder" (6.140). Now it becomes necessary for Tarzan to fight for his life, and he dispatches the gorilla. He is still very puzzled by what is happening and is not sure how to react to these strange phenomena: "If this was a sleep adventure, what then was reality? How was he to know the one from the other? How much of all that had happened in his life had been real and how much unreal?" (6.141). Burroughs' exploration of this question in *Tales* (in chapter 9, "The Nightmare") is not without its share of his prolific humor, but the question is serious and lies at the root of much of ancient Greek philosophy and thought.

If the nightmare makes the thinking Tarzan address himself to the ancient problem of illusion versus reality, an earlier experience in *Tales* forces Tarzan as thinking human being to face the problem of good versus evil (Chapter 4: "The God of Tarzan"). Among the many books he found in his father's cabin was a dictionary, and one day he comes across the word "god." His own conceptual framework leads Tarzan to understand, if dimly, the concept of "god" as "a mighty chieftain, king of all the Mangani (i.e. white men), a great, and all-powerful individual" (6.49). Since the apes can give him no help in this quest, Tarzan tries Mbonga's people. He comes upon a ceremony of passage in which some youths of the village are being promoted to manhood. The witch doctor is present, and because Tarzan does not understand the rituals, "he thought that they must have to do with the God he could not understand" (6.53). The witch doctor proves finally to be a fraud. The whole structure of fakery surrounding the religious activity of the natives reflects Burroughs' thoroughgoing dislike of organized religion in all its forms. (In his *Gods of Mars*, the hero exposes the shameful hustle that organized religion has become on Barsoom.)

After his shame has been revealed, Mbonga's witch doctor attempts to save face by killing Tarzan but fails. Tarzan in turn almost kills the witch doctor, but suddenly stays his hand (6.59).

Somewhat later, Tarzan discovers that somehow Teeka overcomes her fear of Histah the snake so that she can rescue her baby from its coils. Tarzan is puzzled. Why should Teeka "have placed herself within the folds of the horrid monster?" (6.63) Indeed, why did Tarzan risk his life for Teeka's balu? Why had he not killed the old faker who was the witch doctor? Who made the flowers grow? Like ancient cosmogonic speculation, Tarzan's thoughts parallel old formulations of these matters. "Ah, now it was all explained—the flowers, the trees, the moon, the sun, himself, every living creature in the jungle—they were all made by God out of nothing"(6.63).

Tarzan cannot see God, but he adopts the firm conviction that "everything that was good came from God" (6.63): his own hesitation in slaying the witch doctor, Teeka's selfless protection of her infant, his own help in rescuing it, the beauty of nature. To his own immediate satisfaction, he then accounts for the creation of all other things in the jungle, including beautiful Sheeta, noble Numa, and lovely Bara. Like the biblical prophets, he must ask himself about the source of evil or, much as the writers of *Genesis* did some three millennia ago, about where the snake in the garden of Eden came from. "Who made Histah the snake?" (6.64).

The heroic mentality of the classical protagonist is essentially in a state of siege, for it feels threatened by the world at the same time that it must have the world in order to recognize its worth. Burroughs develops this aspect of the heroic personality that involves apartness, separateness, and difference in his portrayal of Tarzan, for Tarzan's general attitudes about other human beings are not, on the whole, favorable, and he sees himself as somehow apart. Even in relationship to the apes, his own "people," he is not always totally comfortable once he reaches thinking age. This apartness is manifested in a number of ways, most notably in his deep-seated misanthropy. Tarzan feels this way towards both animals and men, black and white. When he felt thwarted in his suit of Teeka, for example, he decided to leave the apes, "never to return to the tribe" (6.17), and even after he became king of the apes of Kerchak, he felt he must leave his subjects (1.91).

Tarzan's misanthropic sentiments are also revealed in those synkristic passages in which he is compared to civilized men. In these passages, the romanticized vision of the pure and almost

Edenesque Tarzan parades before the reader in all its noble savagery. There Tarzan's apartness is attributed to his "natural" superiority over the civilized ("corrupted") creatures to whom he is being compared. When, for example, the civilized guests at the outpost to which Tarzan and D'Arnot first come make a wager with Tarzan that he cannot bring down a lion alone, a strong contrast is set up between the nervousness of the men with all their weapons and Tarzan's amused execution of the wager "with the pitiful weapons he had taken" (1.220). Again, it is the savage Tarzan who puts Jane's happiness above his own and "would rather see you happy than to be happy myself" (1.236); the civilized Canler thinks only of his own villainous desires towards Jane and callously disregards her feelings (1.227). In short, Tarzan is not like his civilized brothers.

Shifting our attention to a different aspect of Tarzan's heroicness, we may note that a character's fears and his handling of them offer a not unreasonable touchstone for judging his perceptions of himself and the world in which he moves. Tarzan acquits himself rather well in this respect. He seems to have more of the ever-cautious Odysseus of the *Odyssey* than of the *Iliad* types like Achilles, Patroklos, Hector, Adrestos, and others. For Odysseus is a heroic individual whose strengths lie not so much in his martial prowess as in his cunning and his cautious approach to life. His interest is not primarily in heroic glory or honor, but in pursuing both the pleasures and delights at hand and returning to his mortal wife and home on Ithaca. Odysseus is in better touch with himself, both his strengths and his weaknesses, than the glory-seekers of the *Iliad* and he has lent more than a few of his traits to the persona of Burroughs' Tarzan.

Let us consider the matter of prudence or caution. Odysseus is extremely careful in his encounters with novel situations and strange peoples, for he does not believe in the innate goodness of man. When he meets Nausicaa, for example, he cleverly avoids telling her anything about himself, and yet he manages to gain her trust so that she shows him the way to her father's city. According to Homer, Odysseus told her a "sweet and crafty story" (*Odyssey* 6.148). Only much later, when he has the opportunity to evaluate the land and the people among whom he has been thrown, does he deem it safe to reveal his true identity. Odysseus takes the opposite tack when he encounters Polyphemus, for here Odysseus has correctly diagnosed his host's savagery and tells him only what will pacify him for the moment. When Odysseus does return to Ithaca after twenty years, he displays the same excessive caution even to his wife Penelope before revealing who he is. His disguise as a beggar in part allows him to ferret out the loyal and the disloyal members of the household. After all, his attitude of extreme suspicion has kept him alive while others have perished for rashness and lack of patience.

This characteristic of caution in the Homeric hero is perpetuated in Tarzan, who adopts an attitude of cautious prudence and patience in evaluating new circumstances and alien people. Tarzan's lack of naive trust in strangers probably saved his life the first time he met whites (1.100). Nor does he ever alter the main outlines of his assessment of his human brothers. The contrast between the comportment of Tarzan's son and Tarzan himself under similar circumstances is most instructive. Korak had none of Tarzan's precautionary frame of mind when meeting strange groups (4.52ff., 4.60, 4.68). Korak's very artlessness makes Tarzan's total lack of naiveté the more noteworthy. To the extent that Korak is Telemachus, Tarzan is Odysseus.

In addition to exercising an Odyssean care with strangers, Tarzan has much of Odysseus' cunning and shrewdness. Just as Odysseus' essential cunning keeps him alive on his ten-year journey among savage and unpredictable folk, so Tarzan's "wide . . . cunning" (5.105) enables him to survive the jungle for so many years.

Odysseus takes a cruel revenge on the suitors and the many insolent servants who for years have been living on his wealth and insulting his family. The maidservants who have consorted with the ruinous suitors are unceremoniously hanged from the rafters of the courtyard on Odysseus' orders until "they kept jerking a little while with their feet, and finally not at all" (Odyssey 22.473). The perfidious Melanthius was dragged out into the courtyard for an even less pleasant death (Odyssey 23.475-7). Like the Cyclops, these faithless servants deserve little pity, and the cruelty is somewhat mitigated by the circumstances. Odysseus is, of course, no sentimentalist, and the hard terms of his world allow for few softer sentiments, no possible extenuation, no formal judicial hearings to establish guilt. In his own way he has already determined who is loyal and who is not. As policeman, court, and executioner, Odysseus might be seen as the archetypal fascist, but this view would surely obscure the ethical code and stern conditions under which Homeric life was lived. Odysseus, like all the Homeric heroes, believes that harm is to be done to enemies, and only friends are to be treated benevolently.

Does Tarzan display any of these attitudes? He is not overtly cruel, but cruelty is indeed part of his character. Like Odysseus in the Homeric world, Tarzan in the jungle inhabits a universe that runs largely along popularized Darwinian precepts of survival of the fittest, the most adaptable and the most clever. And survival at times demands what under less rigorous conditions would be gratuitous cruelty.

Tarzan's jungle savagery is best highlighted against the backdrop of an American drawing room. When he arrives in Wisconsin, he learns that Jane is to marry a rich villain named Canler; Tarzan reacts with savage jealousy and acts on it in a way that his more civilized rival for Jane, Clayton, does not. The unfortunate Canler has pressed his suit on Jane with unseemly insistence and is making his way with her to the minister (1.239). Only Jane's urgent pleas with Tarzan prevent him from finishing the job he has begun, and although Tarzan does not understand the notion of sparing one's obvious enemy, he allows Jane to prevail against his jungle code.

In its way, the underlying dynamic of this little scene is very similar to that which operates in the dramatic conclusion of the *Odyssey*. Each hero is fighting for his woman against rival wooers. In the one case (*Odyssey*), the most savage violence and cruel vengeance are condoned by the code of the society. In the other case (*Tarzan*), the problem has become split. One code obtains in the jungle, where Tarzan killed the abducting Terkoz; this action is viewed as appropriate and praiseworthy, for one kills enemies who would harm friends. In civilized society, however, such behavior cannot be condoned, and it is difficult for Tarzan to appreciate the essential difference. Tarzan's Odyssean savagery is sometimes commendable and sometimes forbidden, but it may be seen as part of his Odyssean provenience as a literary figure.

Despite the animal savagery and cruelty in Tarzan, there is also a gentleness in him which differentiates him from his fellows, the apes. Even the savage Odysseus is capable of tender emotions, as when he meets his old dog Argus (*Odyssey* 17.304) or he confronts his wife Penelope and, telling her who he is, is at last accepted by her as the genuine Odysseus (*Odyssey* 23.232). Tarzan's tenderness is explicit amid the savagery and cruelty. "It was not that he was more cruel or more savage than they that hated him, for though he was both cruel and savage as were the beasts, his fellows, yet too was he often tender, which they never were" (6.108).

In the modern terminology, Tarzan is a law-and-order man without having recourse to the endless and tedious irritations of due legal process. It is satisfying, in any age, to identify with a character who can get things done, who has a clear view of what is right and wrong, and who is able to act with genuine impunity to mete out deserved punishment. Few individuals in Tarzan's world enjoy the advantages of plea-bargaining or exoneration on the basis of legal technicalities. No doubt, part of the enormous appeal of a heroic figure like Tarzan is that he can cut through the bureaucratic fat to the bare-boned issues at hand and act accordingly. He is the vicarious embodiment of our deeply rooted desires to exercise intelligent control over our own lives without the meddling interference of governmental "experts" who know what is good for us and the world we inhabit. Delicious as this fantasy is, it must in the final analysis be seen as hopelessly reductive in application to modern "civilized" societies. Vigilantism, social anarchy, and a mindless lawlessness are the inevitable consequences of free-wheeling extralegalism as a means of solving the problem of aberrant behavior, nor does Burroughs advocate them. He draws a distinction between what works in the jungle and what works in civilization in relation to Tarzan's propensity, born of his jungle breeding, to take matters into his own hands.

Vigilantes, even the most justified ones, do have a way of getting out of control, and Burroughs makes it clear that rules must be obeyed in the civilized world, even by Tarzan. In an episode in *Return*, Tarzan has been lured into a trap by a woman pretending to be assaulted by ruffians. Coming to her rescue, the apeman is set upon by thugs whom the villainous Rokoff has hired to kill him. The attackers quickly discover that their victim is no ordinary man, and they are mauled by (in Burroughs' Euripidean phrase) "a veritable Hercules gone mad" (2.28). Rokoff, in a panic that his plan has backfired, calls the local police, reporting that a man is committing murder in the Rue Maule. As the police officers attempt to escort Tarzan to jail, he turns on them in violence and escapes without difficulty. The reader knows that Tarzan was right and that he was merely defending himself. Why should he be hauled off to jail? He will not subject himself to such ridiculous laws (2.29). D'Arnot, alarmed by Tarzan's apparent reluctance to appreciate the authority of the police in civilized society, decides that part of the apeman's education must be an acquaintance with the police. Tarzan cannot be permitted to move about in Paris as a "great child, who could recognize no law mightier than his own mighty physical prowess" (2.32).

At the end of *Return*, Rokoff's bestial behavior to Tarzan's friends compels Tarzan to exact vengeance, but once more Jane prevails upon him to turn the man over to the authorities rather than work his own justice on him. Her analysis of the difference between civilized law and jungle law is not without interest.

"In the heart of the jungle, dear," she said, "with no other form of right or justice to appeal to other than your own mighty muscles, you would be warranted in executing upon this man the sentence he deserves; but with the strong arm of a civilized government at your disposal it would be murder to kill him now. Even your friends would have to submit to your arrest, or if you resisted it would plunge us all into misery and unhappiness again . . ." [2.219].

Tarzan "saw the wisdom of her appeal" (2.219) and surrendered Rokoff to the representatives of the law. Although it goes against his jungle training of killing enemies, the act reveals a Tarzan who is learning, even if not approving of, the customs of civilization. It would appear that Burroughs endorses the apeman's socialization.

A fairly common characterization of Tarzan does speak to this attitude that he has adopted about law and lawgiving. In *Jewels*, it is clear that Tarzan exercises vast influence over the lands under his care, for it is only from him that hunters are given permission to hunt (5.14). A similar point is made in *Son*, where Tarzan's imposition of rules and regulations over a domain that previously had lacked these in fact constitutes a civilizing force. Tarzan's taking of the law into his own hands is not always a question of extralegal behavior but, as here, of setting legal precedent where none existed before. In an age when whites ruled blacks in Africa, Tarzan's concern (though, from today's perspective, patronizing or even humiliating) for the treatment of the blacks by hunters creates an order in that relationship which otherwise was governed by the caprice of one party. His "word was law where there had never been law before" (4.142), and "his word was law among those who hunted within a radius of many miles of his estate" (4.132).

The same novel, *Son*, contains one of those favorite Burroughs passages in which ugly lust is about to spend itself on lovely innocence, only to be thwarted by Tarzan's intercession. The beautiful Meriem is about to be raped by the vicious Swede, Malbihn, when Tarzan comes to the rescue. Meriem informs him of what has been happening and tacitly urges Tarzan to kill Malbihn. Everything Malbihn has done since we first met him on page 40 argues persuasively for the punishment that Meriem's jungle ethic has advocated, but the Tarzan of the fourth novel is a more "civilized" creature than the Tarzan of the earlier novels. After Meriem has made her proposal for Malbihn, the "stranger (viz. Tarzan) smiled. 'He deserves killing?' he said. 'There is no doubt of that. Once I should have killed him; but not now. I will see, though, that he does not bother you any more'" (4.112f.). Tarzan has not given up his jungle code; rather, it has been somewhat tempered by his sojourn among civilized folk. That old code, which in *Beasts* allowed Rokoff to die beneath the grinding jaws of a panther and Schneider to gasp out his last breath with Tarzan's hands on his throat, has its appeal and its usefulness under the right circumstances, but not here. "You deserve death, but I am not the law" (4.113).

The Waziri with whom Tarzan is traveling are also incensed by Malbihn's behavior. Like Meriem, the warrior Muviri suggests that Tarzan should kill Malbihn in payment for the ills Malbihn has worked in and on the jungle. Tarzan is not opposed to the idea, but somewhat wistfully he accepts the passing of the old ways of swift, personal revenge. "'I wish that I might; but a new law is come into this part of the jungle. It is not as it was in the old days, Muviri,' replied the master" (4.115).

Closely related to the notion of Tarzan as an administrator of justice within his domain is that of control. Tarzan exercises control in every sense of the word—on himself, other humans, animals, even enemies. Herein lies a further reason for Tarzan's enormous popularity as a fictional character, for who of us is not from time to time beset by the fraying thought that we are "losing control," be it of ourselves, our own situation in life, or the general ability to order even our private affairs independently of external or internal meddling?[8] In this sense, Tarzan offers a vicarious fantasy.

Tarzan's compelling presence and self-assured control at critical moments show him to be endowed with precisely the qualities most would like to possess. Even on those occasions when things appear to have gone beyond his own personal control, Tarzan is nonetheless able to deal competently and rationally with a disintegrating situation. If external control escapes him at times, internal control is almost always present, and it is manifested as a kind of resigned fatalism of the sort encountered in archaic Greek literature. Man is responsible for his actions and has considerable freedom to live his life as he wishes and make the choices that appeal, but there will be times when, as "things" do not work out and nothing can be done about it, one must simply accept the inevitable as one of the costs of living. It's nothing personal.

Control is a heroic characteristic in Burroughs' heroic world. It is not, however, a noteworthy feature of all Homeric heroes, who, though they can indeed act with speed and conviction, often display paralyzing diffidence about taking action until it is too late. Some, like Odysseus, have little difficulty in formulating quick plans of action and acting on these with haste, but others, like Achilles, brood and mull over things interminably or until such action as is forthcoming comes forth too late to prevent unhappy consequences. Tarzan clearly falls into the Odyssean category, for he has great decisiveness and control. He does not sit back and wait for things to happen before he acts, but meets the problem head on while there is still time for useful deeds.

Not much has been said hitherto about the characteristics commonly ascribed to Tarzan throughout the novels, but the discussions above give a fair and accurate view of Tarzan's position in a tradition that stretches back to Homeric prototypes. He has the physical prowess of an Achilles and the cunning of an Odysseus; he has the propensity for murderous anger, conceives grand hatreds, can love with tenderness, and has the ability to remain cool and calm in extreme dangers; he is susceptible to bitterness and depression but has a sparkling sense of humor; his insane jealousies and envy are balanced by deep loyalties and astonishing self-sacrifice; set against his fatalistic indifference to death in its many cruel manifestations is a strong and vibrant belief in life; his infinite patience can become a petulant impatience; his stoic front can mask extreme sensitivity; a sometimes necessary cruelty can turn into compassion; what may appear as his ingenuousness in civilization has great survival value in the jungle; a preoccupation with himself and his own merits is at times countered by genuine humility and embarrassed self-depreciation; a serious and stern streak in his makeup answers to an almost frivolous engagement in practical jokes and pranksterism; capable of deep emotion on all levels, he may sometimes seem inhumanly phlegmatic in his attitudes to others; infinitely flexible and inventive, he is simultaneously stubborn and persistent; of a contemplative and thoughtful frame of mind, he is also openly contemptuous of many of civilization's ways; though a beast he is a man; though highly prideful over his self-sufficiency, he is subject to loneliness and strong needs for companionship—in short, Tarzan of the Apes, like most heroic types, is a bewildering and complicated mix of polar thoughts, emotions, attitudes, and beliefs. He contains multitudes.

A final characteristic that requires examination in this chapter is the whole complex of Tarzan's humor, practical joking, and trickster-like behavior. It is a prominent aspect of his persona and one that further defines his literary provenience. Here one must acknowledge not only the classical component, but also Burroughs' documented familiarity with American Indians and Indian culture, both of which played productive roles in the creation of "trickster Tarzan."

A standard work on the type among American Indians is the study by Paul Radin, in which he concentrates on the particular trickster figure among the Winnebago Indians of central Wisconsin and eastern Nebraska.[9] As Radin reports, the myth-cycle that deals with the exploits of the trickster "is an old cultural possession of all the American Indians."[10] Indeed, the trickster is a universal mythic type, tied down in neither time nor space.

The Trickster myth is found in clearly recognizable form among the simplest aboriginal tribes and among the complex. We encounter it among the ancient Greeks, the Chinese, the Japanese and in the Semitic world. Many of the Trickster's traits were perpetuated in the figure of the mediaeval jester, and have survived right up to the present day in the Punch-and-Judy plays and in the clown. Although repeatedly combined with other myths and frequently drastically reorganized and reinterpreted, its basic plot seems always to have succeeded in reasserting itself.[11]

Burroughs does not adopt the total personality of trickster in his Tarzan but is selective, emphasizing some of the trickster's features and deemphasizing others. It is not to be assumed that he went only to Indian material for the development of his literary trickster, for many of the patterns Tarzan displays are closer to those in ancient literature, and some of the practices of the Amerindian tricksters are lacking in Tarzan. Trickster Tarzan appears to be a composite of classical and Amerindian tricksters, if not of many others familiar to Burroughs from his extensive reading.

According to Radin, the trickster type as he appears among the Winnebagos is close to nature and is in touch with its creatures in a way that far transcends the average person's awareness of it. The trickster can converse with animals and they with him, for they understand each other. The Winnebago trickster shares another common feature of the general type in that he "operates outside the fixed bounds of custom and law," and he is "at the same time creator and destroyer." The trickster has certain problems identifying himself precisely and defining himself in the social context, and despite initial difficulties in attempts to socialize him, he does end up marrying, raising a son, and assuming the standard obligations that befall any responsible member of a social group. Although he can be very destructive and negative in his views to humans, he can also be very helpful; indeed he becomes a benefactor. He functions as a kind of culture hero, another mythic type well established among the ancient Greeks, Amerindians, and many other cultures. Although not all tricksters are theriomorphic, the Amerindian (and many African) tricksters are decidedly so. Common forms include the hare, raven, coyote, and spider. Furthermore, the trickster is seen, at least on Radin's reading of the Winnebago cycle, as a paradigmatic figure whose evolution and development are meant to articulate identical experiences among the members of the tribe. The trickster is an extremely clever and cunning individual—so much so that he often outsmarts himself and gets into serious difficulties.[12]

These characteristics are familiar from Tarzan's persona. Tarzan is not a complete trickster, however, but rather an example of what Radin calls a "partial" trickster.[13] Tarzan lacks some of the prominent characteristics of the type, such as a gluttonous abandonment to the physical appetites (a form of behavior that specifically disgusts Tarzan—cf. 6.130f.) and the consuming sexuality of the Winnebago trickster. While Tarzan is unquestionably a creature of enormous sexual attraction, the motif has undergone severe muting in Burroughs' hero.

One of the most consistent features in the trickster-cycle of myth and legend is the joke or prank that backfires on the trickster. It is the time when he has proved too clever for his own good, and he falls into great danger. Let us take an example from Tarzan's life. After Mamka is killed by Numa (6.123), Tarzan institutes a sentry system among the apes to watch for the approach of enemies while the rest of the tribe feeds or amuses itself. This very act of teaching the society of apes such a novel institution qualifies Tarzan as the culture-hero type in that he is bringing to the group a means for improving its collective life. The procedure works very well, and the apes are satisfied with the decrease in excitement which the sentry system affords. Tarzan, however, grows restless with the predictable security the tribe now enjoys from his innovation.

But Tarzan went abroad alone, for Tarzan was a man-thing and sought amusement and adventure and such humor as the grim and terrible jungle offers to those who know it and do not fear it—a weird humor shot with blazing eyes and dappled with the crimson of lifeblood [6.124].

Tarzan comes to the village of Mbonga and witnesses the witch doctor performing a dance while dressed in the hide and head of Gorgo the buffalo. The dance gives Tarzan an idea. Later that night, he returns to the village and steals the mane and skin of

Numa the lion. He decks himself out in this disguise and pretends to be Numa approaching the grounds of the apes in order to attack them. Tarzan does so in order to prove to the apes the necessity for maintaining their vigilance, for he "was confident that they had ceased to place the watchers about them the moment that he had left them" (6.126). The trickster's trickery backfires, however, and almost kills him. Tarzan has underestimated the apes, who did in fact have guards posted, and they were attentive enough to Tarzan's admonitions that they actually did take note of the comings and goings of possible enemies. When the "lion" appears, the apes' reaction to the warning shrieks of the guard is instantaneous. The haughty intruder is met with a barrage of missiles and so ferociously attacked that the animal, alias Tarzan, falls down unconscious (6.127). If Manu the monkey had not been privy to Tarzan's trickery, the outcome might indeed have been most unfortunate for the apeman. But Manu attracts the attention of the apes and succeeds in pulling off Tarzan's disguise. Some apes want to finish the job begun, but loyal Manu and other friends among the apes themselves prevent the killing. When Tarzan returns to consciousness, he is delighted to have discovered who his friends are and to have learned that the apes did heed his lessons about maintaining guards against intruders. Although he appreciates the comic aspects of his experiment, it does give him cause to reflect.

It made Tarzan glad to know these things; but at the other lesson he had been taught he reddened. He had always been a joker, the only joker in the grim and terrible company; but now as he lay there half dead from his hurts, he almost swore a solemn oath forever to forego practical joking—almost; but not quite [6.128].

The concluding tag typifies the attitude of the trickster, who can no more give up his prankish ways than he can stop breathing.

Several incidents in this episode recall earlier prototypes of the trickster-figure, especially Odysseus. Like Tarzan, Odysseus frequently employs disguises and prevarications to hide his true self from those he is testing. The whole sequence of Odysseus' disguise as a beggar when he returns to Ithaca is a rather straightforward example of the same thing. He wishes to test the loyalty of the members of his household and can do so only by appearing as someone other than himself. So, too, Tarzan learns who his friends and enemies are as a result of his disguise in the lionskin. In the manner of Odysseus' return to his home, there is also the ancillary element of the test, the examination of his group to see if they are carrying on appropriately. On the journey of return from Troy, Odysseus has tried to guide his men and establish procedures that might lead to their own salvation—one thinks here especially of his efforts to have them behave safely on the Island of the Sun (*Odyssey* 12.134ff., 19.273ff.).

Just as Tarzan intends to help his community by providing a system of security against predators and disruptors of the group, so Odysseus tries by his deceit to cleanse his world of usurpers and freeloaders in order to restore some order to a chaotic household. Tarzan's doings, though presented in a humorous vein by Burroughs, are nonetheless fully comprehensible in the traditional framework of the trickster-type who is also the culture hero. Finally, to expect that the protagonist would be sufficiently chastened by his near escape from a death he has devised for himself is, of course, to misapprehend the essence of the trickster, and Burroughs' final words on the subject show that he appreciated the point fully. Whether consciously or intuitively, Burroughs has a firm grasp on the conventions of the tradition.

Another passage in *Tales* underlines the trickster element in Tarzan and at the same time demonstrates the contribution of the Amerindian heritage to the construction of Burroughs' world. The passage in question is Tarzan's rescue of the moon.

Once Tarzan had observed how a group of black warriors stranded in the jungle for the night had built a huge fire in their camp in order to keep away the prowling cats and other predators who would attack them. The sheen of the fire had illuminated the jungle night with pinpoints of light reflecting from the eyes of various animals that circled the camp. Later, on the basis of this experience, Tarzan posits a reasonable explanation for the stars in the nocturnal sky. Tarzan is so excited by his discovery that he wakes up Taug in the middle of the night to explain (6.181). His account, interesting in its own right as suggestive of Burroughs' adaptation of theories current in his day about the mythmaking capacities of "primitive" peoples on the basis of the observation of natural phenomena, sets up the novel's climactic display by Tarzan of a cunning so powerful as to make him forever a living legend among the apes, "for now the apes looked up to him as a superior being" (6.191). The passage presents Tarzan to us in an unsurpassable tour de force of control and domination over a situation that has cosmic implications for the universe in which he lives with the apes and other animals.

One night after Tarzan has left the tribe to go to his cabin, his ape-friend Taug lay looking up at the sky, wondering about the vivid picture Tarzan had once painted for him of animals stalking the fields of heaven in ceaseless predation on Goro the moon. The implications of Tarzan's narrative disturb the ape very much.

And then a strange thing happened. Even as Taug looked at Goro, he saw a portion of one edge disappear, precisely as though something was gnawing upon it. Larger and larger became the hole in the side of Goro. With a scream, Taug leaped to his feet. His frenzied "Kreeg-ahs!" brought the terrified tribe screaming and chattering toward him.

"Look!" cried Taug, pointing to the moon. "Look! It is as Tarzan said. Numa has sprung through the fires and is devouring Goro. You called Tarzan names and drove him from the tribe; now see how wise he was. Let one of you who hated Tarzan go to Goro's aid. See the eyes in the dark jungle all about Goro. He is in danger and none can help him—none except Tarzan. Soon Goro will be devoured by Numa and we shall have no more light after Kudu (viz. the sun) seeks his lair. How shall we dance the Dum-Dum without the light of Goro?"

The apes trembled and whimpered. Any manifestation of the powers of nature always filled them with terror, for they could not understand [6.189].

Taug rushes off in desperate haste to fetch Tarzan from the cabin, for only Tarzan offers any hope of salvation for the doomed apes. Tarzan comes quickly, and, clambering up into the topmost branches of a tree, he begins to shoot arrows at the ferocious monster who is gobbling up Goro before their very eyes (6.190).

Whether Tarzan knew what he was doing is hardly the point here, but this supernatural bluff by the great trickster establishes a strong likelihood that Burroughs was familiar with an account of the

Apaches of the Southwestern United States. This account is filled with physical descriptions of the Apaches' great endurance, skill at mimicking animals when decked out in their hides, wiliness and cruelty in a cruel domain, and many other points that have a bearing on the protrayal of Tarzan as hero.

What was Burroughs' source for this story about Tarzan's rescue of the moon? One can only speculate.[14] It is known that he did conduct research for his stories,[15] and since he wrote Westerns and Indian stories, it is reasonable to assume that he did considerable reading in this area. In addition, he had personal experience of the Southwest from his days in the cavalry. Clearly, many of the things he read about Indians were transferred to his portrait of Tarzan. One book in particular stands out as a likely source for the Amerindian contribution to his fictional hero: John C. Cremony's account, published in 1868, of his years in the American Southwest as a member of the U.S. Boundary Commission prior to the Civil War and his subsequent sojourn in Arizona as captain of the California Volunteer Cavalry. Cremony was an interpreter and a keen observer of the customs of the Indians, mainly the Apaches and Comanches, whom he encountered in various official capacities.[16] The book is almost Herodotean in sweep and anecdotal particularity, and represents fascinating reading in its own right. Pertinent to the discussion at hand is the publisher's comment in a prefatory note to a limited edition put out in 1951: "This rare book has been one of the most important source books *among writers* and historians from the date of its first publication." [Italics added] Indeed, in reading Cremony's intriguing account of the Indian way of life before the white man destroyed their established customs (a point Cremony himself commented on with some bitterness over a hundred years ago),[17] one is reminded of certain characteristics imputed to Tarzan. The connection cannot, of course, be proved, barring a revelation that Burroughs had read Cremony's book, but the likelihood is strong. The validity of this supposition is reenforced by the account Cremony gives of an event in which some white men "rescued" the moon and as a result probably saved themselves from massacre by a band of hostile Indians.

Cremony had been invited on an expedition organized for the express purpose of observing an eclipse of the moon. Several hundred Indians belonging to the Pimos (whom Cremony designated as among "the most superstitious") and Maricopas displayed intense curiosity about the telescopes and other paraphernalia the group was carting up a hill. Cremony offhandedly told them that it was a cannon with which the moon would be shot. Unfortunately, as the moon did go into eclipse, the Indians grew very agitated and fearful, and threatened to attack. Cremony recorded the chief's frantic questions:

"What are we to do without the moon?" inquired the Chief. "How are we to note time? How shall we know when to plant and when to reap? How can we pass all our nights in darkness, and be incapacitated from preventing Apache raids? What have we done to you, that you should do this thing to us?"[18]

One compares Taug's comment to the bewildered apes: " '. . . and we shall have no more light after Kudu seeks his lair. How shall we dance the Dum-Dum without the light of Goro? (6.189). Both leaders are concerned that the disappearance of the moon will interrupt the tribe's important ceremonial and life-sustaining activities.

The man in charge of the expedition, Whipple, informed Cremony that he should tell the chief that they had wanted to destroy the moon in order to prevent the Pimos' enemies, the Apaches, from sneaking up on them, but since the Pimos would rather have the moon than security, he would in fact restore the moon—but only if they promised not to cause difficulties or attack the vastly outnumbered party of white men. The chief kept a troubled peace among his excited people, but when in due course the eclipse came to an end, the Indians were delirious with happiness.

To describe the joy, the amazement and the homage of the savages is quite impossible. We were lifted up on their arms, patted on our backs, embraced, and dignified to their utmost extent. All this time Mr. Whipple had been quietly taking his observations and writing them in his book. At no period did he appear ruffled or concerned. His equanimity won respect, and his influence with the Pimos became all powerful.[19]

Compare Burroughs' droll description of the aftermath of Tarzan's rescue of the moon, which also forms the conclusion of *Tales.*

At last came a cry from Taug. "Look!" he screamed. "Numa is killed. Tarzan has killed Numa . . ." . . . were you to try to convince an ape of the tribe of Kerchak that it was aught but Numa who so nearly devoured Goro that night, or that another than Tarzan preserved the brilliant god of their savage and mysterious rites from a frightful death, you would have difficulty—and a fight on your hands.

And so Tarzan of the Apes came back to the tribe of Kerchak, and in his coming he took a long stride toward the kingship, which he ultimately won, for now the apes looked up to him as a superior being.

In all the tribe there was but one who was at all skeptical about the plausibility of Tarzan's remarkable rescue of Goro, and that one, strange as it may seem, was Tarzan of the Apes [6.190f.].

The cool self-possession of Whipple, the astronomer and leader of the white party, impressed both the Indians and Cremony, who comments several times on it in the course of his account. It does not seem farfetched to suggest a direct relationship between this story in Cremony's book and Burroughs' narrative. Nor should one think that the connection, if it is genuine, is in any sense indicative of Burroughs' auctorial underhandedness. He borrows extensively from the past and adapts the material to his own ends, and the point in introducing this one parallel narrative is simply to underscore the eclectic origins of Tarzan.

Little doubt can exist about the profoundly classical mold in which Tarzan and the whole *mythos* of his universe have been poured, but this fact should not blind us to other contributory influences. While there are, of course, earlier American, English, and continental antecedents to Burroughs' works, in this book the primary concern is to demonstrate the overridingly powerful sway of the classical Greek and Roman tradition as well as to indicate that a purely native American tradition may also be present in both characterization and narrative. At the same time, one ought not to speak of some factitious alloying of indigenous Americana and classical literature to fashion a new product more vigorous than either component. The classical contribution is by far the most pervasive and authoritative one, but it does not stand alone. The native American contribution, though it may perhaps be more literary than anthropologically accurate, nonetheless merits its due consideration in this very American author.

Be that as it may, Tarzan the hero can be understood as an outgrowth of both traditions: as a classical combination of body (the doer of deeds) and mind (the speaker of words) with its Odyssean overtones of craftiness, and as the Amerindian (and classical and universal) trickster hero. Tarzan is a completely legitimate heir to the literary and mythic origins discussed here.

THEMES

_____ 5 _____

If we comment on an author's use of language and style, his employment of various techniques, or his portrayal of characters, we still do not have a firm grasp on what it is that an author is *saying* in his works. Only by turning to the themes do we come to a fuller recognition of these matters. What are the important themes of the Tarzan novels? What are the central and dominating ideas, concepts, or theses that inform and organize the novels? Let us first consider the theme of the erotic and its subspecies. The idea of an erotic hero is ancient, antedating Homer by countless generations. It is already fully and masterfully developed in Homer and is linked closely to physical violence—a combination that appears to enjoy a venerable antiquity. The Trojan War, a brief portion of which is the setting for Homer's *Iliad*, was fought over a woman, Helen. Eroticism is also a prominent theme in Burroughs.

Tarzan's first awareness of his sexuality is explicitly tied to the story of the Trojan War and Helen, whose passions brought death to so many heroes. In the opening chapter of *Tales*, the novel that more than any of the other six novels under scrutiny here deals with the education of Tarzan into an adult understanding of the world, Burroughs presents the archetypal triangle, two males and one female. Burroughs maintains a finely poised equilibrium between humor and the underlying seriousness of the depiction of a youth's first sexual stirrings.

The beautiful female ape Teeka has discovered that she can excite
the jealous competition of the ape Taug and the white-skin, Tarzan, for both stalwarts have deep feelings for her. The principals
come to blows over her, and engage in a terrifying battle. The
paragraph that interests us most immediately is the one in which
Burroughs describes Teeka's reaction to the battle that is being
fought in her honor.

The spurt of red blood brought a shrill cry of delight from Teeka. Ah, but
this was something worth while! She glanced about to see if others had
witnessed this evidence of her popularity. *Helen of Troy was never one
whit more proud than was Teeka at that moment* [6.11, italics added].

The notion of a basic conflict between two men or women over
one woman or man appears not only in Homer but also later as a
core theme in the so-called New Comedy of both Greek and Roman
literature, and it flourishes as a standard conceit in the amatory
poetry of the Roman elegists of the late republic and early empire. In
the enormously popular "romances" of later Greek literature, the
melodramatic complications of countless heroines at the hands of
swarthy villains are a natural outgrowth of the treatment of the
theme during the previous millennium, and it is this late blossom-
ing of the theme that comes closest to Burroughs' handling of it.[1]
From Homer's *Iliad* and *Odyssey* to Heliodorus' *Aethiopica*, a
period covering roughly a millennium, we meet all the love-related
rescues, villains, perils, shipwrecks, abductions, marvels, saga-
fantasies, strange cities and stranger peoples, mistaken identities,
complicated forms of passion, and spectacular plotting that are so
dear to Burroughs. Few themes in Burroughs' works are more firmly rooted in the fertile soil of classical literature than the erotic
ones.
     Tarzan's sexuality is never explicitly explored, but it is
nonetheless highly visible. Burroughs' powerful evocation of it
derives precisely from suggestion, teasing allusiveness, and
allowance for the reader's fantasy. As an example, we may cite the
passage that describes Tarzan's and Jane's first night alone in the
jungle after her rescue from the lusting ape Terkoz. Tarzan, suspec-
ting that Jane is concerned about her safety, apparently interprets

her worry as one based on sex. Throughout this sojourn with the rescued girl Tarzan has been presented as quite aware of his own sexual desires and cognizant of the fact that the males of the jungle have but one code in this matter (1.163). Burroughs' portrayal of their going to sleep, she within the little hut that he has made for her and he on the ground immediately "at the entrance to her bower" (1.169), is a masterpiece of phallic symbolism.

> So Tarzan of the Apes did the only thing he knew to assure Jane of her safety. He removed his hunting knife from its sheath and handed it to her hilt first, again motioning her into the bower.
>
> The girl understood, and taking the long knife she entered and lay down upon the soft grasses while Tarzan of the Apes stretched himself upon the ground across the entrance.
>
> And thus the rising sun found them in the morning [1.169].

An ancillary erotic theme is that of abduction. It is pervasive in the Tarzan novels, and Terkoz is the first of many villains pressed into its mold. Terkoz, Tarzan's foster brother, has always been hostile towards him. After the ape has been humiliated by Tarzan (1.91-94) and expelled from the tribe (1.152), he wanders aimlessly in the jungle and comes upon Jane. His lust to kill is replaced by a different lust, and the scene is swiftly eroticized. As he is pulling Jane towards him to bury his fangs in her throat,

> ere they touched that fair skin another mood claimed the anthropoid.
>
> The tribe had kept his women. He must find others to replace them. This hairless white ape would be the first of his new household, and so he threw her roughly across his broad, hairy shoulders and leaped back into the trees, bearing Jane away [1.153].

We are never given any further details about Terkoz' designs on Jane Porter, but eroticism clearly is primary in the abduction. What Terkoz might do to Jane is left to the reader's imagination. The somewhat bizarre implications of Terkoz' abduction point to Burroughs' fondness for the grotesque, especially in the erotic scenes, not only in the Tarzan novels but also in the Martian series and some of the other fiction. The juxtaposition of incommensurates that has been observed in the Terkoz scene is a common way for

Burroughs to highlight his sense for the grotesque. In *Jewels*, for example, it looks for a while as though Jane will be sold into a lifetime of servitude in a Moslem harem (5.11, 5.52); and in the same novel she becomes a seemingly helpless object of the erotic attentions of the vile Mohammed Beyd (5.125ff.) and the enraged ape Taglat (5.101f.). There is also an incident in which Jane has to confront a hungry lion, and the scene is written with a fine sense for erotic double-entendres (5.118). The grotesque amatory designs of gorilla-like Tha on the exquisite La (2.169ff.) also makes for an interesting example of this preoccupation by Burroughs, as do the repeated attempts in *Son* on innocently youthful Meriem by such grotesque villains as a bull ape (4.84ff.), a degenerate Swede (4.110), and a warped Arab (4.204). And the very notion of Tarzan in love with the she-ape Teeka is rather grotesque if pursued to a logical amatory conclusion. Here again one should observe that the great Tarzan artist Burne Hogarth has captured the essence of this aspect of Burroughs' literary portrayal in his own strongly expressionistic accentuation of gnarled landscape forms and contorted figure anatomy that is at times in bizarre defiance of realistically possible poses.

The passage discussed above also provides another example of the eternal triangle which Burroughs, like Homer, so loved. To the specific triangle of Teeka-Taug-Tarzan and Jane-Clayton-Tarzan we may now add that of Jane-Terkoz-Tarzan. The inevitable battle between rivals ensues, and this time Tarzan does not let Terkoz live. The struggle itself is cast in terms quite similar to those in which Teeka had conceived of the fight for herself by Taug and Tarzan, although in the present conflict there are phylogenetic overtones.

Jane—her lithe, young form flattened against the trunk of a great tree, her hands tight pressed against her rising and falling bosom, and her eyes wide with mingled horror, fascination, fear and admiration—watched the primordial ape battle with the primeval man for possession of a woman—of her [1.155f.].

Another example occurs at 3.68. The evil Russian villain Rokoff has taken Jane away on the same ship that brought her husband to

Jungle Island, where he was abandoned, and only a few days later Rokoff makes his proposal of marriage to Jane (3.68). Her cool rebuff ignites his rage, and like "a wild beast he sprang upon her, and with his strong fingers at her throat forced her backward upon the berth" (3.69).

The tantalizing possibilities of this scene are cut short by the interruption of the Swedish cook, Anderssen, who helps Jane escape from Rokoff, but later she falls into Rokoff's clutches once more. In one of his rages Rokoff attacks Jane, and although she fights back, he drags her to the cot in his tent where he tries to rape her (3.100f.). The rapist's desires are thwarted by Jane herself, who gets his gun, knocks him out with it, and manages to escape. After further peril she, Rokoff, and Tarzan once more come together on board the ship *Kincaid*, which had carried them to Africa at the beginning of the novel. It is here that Tarzan's panther devours the evil Russian, and he ceases to be a threat to Tarzan and his family.

Rokoff's abduction of Jane allows a basis for generalization about the typical pattern of the theme. The most obvious point is that Terkoz is an animal, a beast, and that this designation is exactly the one applied to Rokoff in the simile at 3.69. The human concept of raping a lovely innocent is attributed to the beast Terkoz, and the bestialization of the human Rokoff imparts to him characteristics of a Terkoz. The worst elements of each is brought out; the theme is an aspect of the beauty-and-the-beast, and in Burroughs' world it is not only beasts who are beastly.

Just as Terkoz questioned Tarzan's control over the apes through his kingships, so Rokoff is enraged at Tarzan because of Tarzan's attempt to exercise control over his schemes against Olga de Coude and others. Rokoff's frustrations over setbacks and humiliations suffered at Tarzan's hands parallel Terkoz's rage for the same reasons, and both villains delight in the prospect of obtaining revenge through Jane. Like Terkoz who imagines that he will establish a new family all by himself in the jungle and take Jane as his first mate (1.153), so, too, Rokoff spins out exaggerated fantasies of his power and sexual attractiveness to Jane.

Two final points remain about these villains and their roles in the erotic theme. First, both are social misfits. Terkoz planned violence against his fellows and was expelled from the community, and Rokoff, because of a "scandal" (2.37), was cashiered from the Russian army and consorted with criminal types of every persuasion. Second, the element of the grotesque appears in both instances of this erotic theme of abduction. The grotesque idea of Jane's rape by Terkoz requires no further elaboration, and Rokoff's plans are almost as grim. When Rokoff is rebuffed by Jane, he decides that she is to be enslaved to a cannibal chief to become one of his concubines and bear him children. If she will not have the cultured refinement of civilized life that he so nobly has offered her, she shall sink into hopeless barbarism.

In summary, the following outline of typical motifs associated with the theme may be useful.

1. Villain is somehow a beast, in fact or in intent.
2. Villain resents Tarzan's interference.
3. Villain seeks revenge on Tarzan through those closest to him.
4. Villain is a coward and a bully.
5. Villain is hybristic, coming to a bad end because of his hybris.
6. Villain is an outcast, does not fit in a society or social group.
7. An element of the grotesque is present.
8. Rescue is effected by Tarzan or through his intercession.

Not every episode in which Jane (or some other woman, for example Meriem several times in *Son*) is abducted contains all of these motifs. An examination of a larger sampling would reveal ancillary motifs, but this pattern is a basic core on which all such passages are constructed according to formula. The entire business is quite Homeric in conception,[2] and this erotic subtheme of abduction, of course, has its most famous antecedent in the Paris-Helen story.

Of the many women who become enamored of Tarzan, including the young she-ape Teeka, none is more passionate than the beautiful La, priestess of Opar. La, as the very name suggests, is, like Kala, the quintessentially feminine She, though representing a different aspect of the feminine from Kala. La's beauty is exquisite and her passions enormous; she has qualities of both Circe and Medea. Her rage and lust for vengeance when she is rejected are awesome. The following characterization of La and her background is not without its Ovidian preciosity.

The coming of Tarzan had aroused within La's breast the wild hope that at last the fulfillment of this ancient prophecy was at hand; but more strongly still had it aroused the hot fires of love in a heart that never otherwise would know the meaning of that all-consuming passion. . . . She had grown to young womanhood a cold and heartless creature, daughter of a thousand other cold, heartless, beautiful women who had never known love. And so when love came to her it liberated all the pent passions of a thousand generations, transforming La into a pulsing, throbbing volcano of desire, and with desire thwarted this great force of love and gentleness and sacrifice was transmuted by its own fires into one of hatred and revenge [5.65].

In *Return*, La is twice disappointed in her desire to keep Tarzan with her. The time separating this incident from their next meeting in *Jewels* must be at least twenty years, for in the interim Tarzan has married and his son Jack has grown up and married (4.219), presumably at the same age as his father. Nonetheless, both Tarzan and La (in their early forties at this time?) are as desirable as ever, and we learn that for these twenty years La has gone against the dictates of her religion and her assigned role in her society (that she marry one of the ugly Oparian men—see 2.173f., 5.65) by waiting for Tarzan's return. La's flouting of the norms of her world is Ovidian in its grotesqueness, and in her own way she is the literary descendant of Ovid's foolish Thisbe, insane Medea, vacillating Myrrha, and raging Ariadne, to mention a few. La's love is an obsession, an unhealthy thing in the best tradition of the great classical passions, and she offers Tarzan heaven and earth if he will but stay (5.41). After these impassioned protestations of her enduring and eternal love, one may well imagine how easily love is transformed into hate, especially in view of Tarzan's reply to her. "The ape-man pushed the kneeling woman aside. 'Tarzan does not desire you,' he said, simply" (5.41). This erotic antihero is reminiscent of all those heroic protagonists who shun their insanely passionate women in Ovid and earlier Hellenistic poets such as Theocritus and Apollonius, and La's outraged reaction is true to the Ovidian form. Even Burroughs'extravagant prose to describe her wrath recalls the stylistic preciosity in which Ovid's Latin wraps the diatribes of his abandoned heroines.

Beneath this Ovidian patina we find the erotic relationship of the Homeric Odysseus with various females. The great witch Circe, for example, has more than a few points of contact with La. The passage on the prophecy that La knew (5.65) about the coming of someone like her Atlantean ancestors is reminiscent of Hermes' prophecy to Circe regarding Odysseus.

Surely you are Odysseus of many turns; Hermes the bearer of the golden wand and the slayer of Argos always kept telling me that you would come when you were on your way back from Troy in your swift, dark ship (*Odyssey* 10.330ff.).

Nor is the great power which La exercises in her capacity as high priestess without its elements of witchery, ritual, and religious humbug (2.184). Circe, too, knows more than witchcraft, for she has precise knowledge of the religious rituals Odysseus must undertake before he can enter the world of the dead. It is perhaps no coincidence that La, correspondingly, guides her hero down into the ancient Chamber of the Dead (2.183f.), much as Circe's instructions guided Odysseus to the Land of the Dead. For both heroes their encounter with bewitchingly beautiful ladies becomes the ultimate means of escape from a kingdom of death. Any reader of Tarzan's escape from the Chamber of the Dead will readily appreciate the symbolic value of the darkness, the endless caverns and secret passages in the heroic *katabasis* and subsequent *anabasis*. Burroughs gives the literate reader a clear indication of the classical provenience of this passage when he informs us that where "Tarzan stood it was dark as Erebus" (2.184).

Why does Tarzan reject La in *Jewels*? It is partly because he is an "upright" hero who would not engage in an extramarital affair and partly because he has now been married a long time to Jane and is committed to her in his heart. Tarzan's attitude must also be viewed as an adaptation of a cardinal feature of his Odyssean prototype. In the *Odyssey*, the hero Odysseus is very much an erotic hero, albeit at times reluctant, at the same time that he is deeply committed to Penelope.

The allure of the goddess Calypso (*Odyssey* 5.206ff.) is similar to that which La displayed before Tarzan when she asked that he not leave her (5.41). La cannot give Tarzan immortality, but she offers temptations much like those Odysseus is offered. Odysseus is too much a man of *this* world, too realistic about himself and his own predicament, to be led astray by Calypso's seductive proposals. He knows his own passions too well, and in the sexual realm they center squarely on his wife. No matter what tribulations the attempt to return may entail, he will undergo them. Penelope is only mortal, and Calypso immortal and ageless, but his wife's very mortality and humanness make her preferable. Tarzan, in rejecting all the promises that beautiful La dangles before him, is a rather obvious adaptation of the type Odysseus represents. As erotic hero, Tarzan is part of that tradition in which the hero resists the seductress' attempts to divert him from the "right" course.

Tarzan's resolve is not always as forceful, for on at least one occasion he begins to yield to his passionate nature. Manipulated by his foe Rokoff into arriving at Olga de Coude's apartments when her husband is absent, Tarzan is puzzled to learn that she had not sent for him. Olga immediately senses Rokoff's evil hand in these immodest arrangements, and she is stunned at the realization of what Rokoff is planning. Her eyes take on, in Burroughs' Ovidian phrasing, the "expression that the hunter sees in those of a poor, terrified doe" (2.44).

As in Ovid, so in Burroughs the illicit tryst is not told for its purely erotic or semipornographic evocations but rather to make a point. Ovid's tendency, in addition to the frequent tag of metamorphosis, is primarily to suggest that reason is helpless when confronted with the raging forces of sexual passion, and, at least in the affair of Olga de Coude, Burroughs' use of the theme seems to promote a similar view. We do not know what might have happened, for the count interrupts the passionate couple *flagrante osculo* as it were, and his attack on Tarzan with his walking stick elicits a primordial response. For once, absolutely beside himself and beyond self-control, Tarzan is metamorphosed into a raging beast ("each blow aided in the transition of the ape-man back to the primordial"—2.45) who springs upon the terrified count and almost kills him before coming to his senses. Events are not allowed to go to the fatal extremes that Ovid relishes, but Tarzan is clearly conscious of great "sorrow and contrition" (2.45) for what he has done to the count as a result of a foolish infatuation.

Although parts of this entire episode are played for laughs, much as is the individual case in Ovid, there is, again as in Ovid, an underlying seriousness to the whole affair. Tarzan explains that he does not understand women because he has not had much experience with them (2.49). Part of the education of any hero is the confrontation with his sexuality and his learning to master it so that it does not master him in turn. At this time Tarzan has been out of the jungle only "a little more than a year" (2.46), and, before Olga, his single experience of woman has been Jane. No hero is born with the knowledge of how to deal with his sexuality, and Tarzan is no exception. In this respect, he comes closest among the classical heroes to Vergil's Aeneas, who must also learn, painfully, the proper role sex is to play in his life.

Suppose, for example, that La's overtly sexual advances to Tarzan in *Jewels* (5.70) had come when he was not a mature fortyish but a youthful twenty-two, as he was in the affair with Olga. Even the torrid passage in *Jewels* with its humorously presented rejection of La does have its more serious purpose. Here Tarzan is a mature hero who, like the mature Odysseus (whose age in the *Odyssey* must be in the early forties), knows with absolute conviction what he wants in the matter of sex—his wife.[3]

The erotic theme is manifested not only in the subtypes examined above but also in a kind of implied synkrisis; in addition to the villains in pursuit of the fair lady, there are "decent" rivals who compete avidly with the apeman. The most prominent of these is William Cecil Clayton, Lord Greystoke, Tarzan's first cousin. The erotic parallelism in their pursuits of Jane Porter is underscored by the ties of blood that join them, and, in the sustained synkrisis between the two men, Burroughs defines the erotic hero more closely (cf. 1.111, 113, 119f.).

When Jane is abducted by Terkoz, Clayton tries to discover a clue about her disappearance, but again, he is pitifully incapable of productive action. His reactions are noble and correct, but, as Burroughs seems to be saying repeatedly through his characterization of Clayton, intentions are not worth much unless supported by useful deeds. In contrast to Clayton and his bumbling attempts to find Jane, Tarzan rescues her by killing the abductor, the ape Terkoz.

Unlike the typical story in which boy meets girl, in Burroughs' tale Tarzan does not win his Jane at the conclusion of the novel. The last twenty pages of *Tarzan* are fraught with complications, erotic triangles, confusion, and, alas, Tarzan's failure to win his suit. But a romance with all the comedic strains of *Tarzan* needs to end in marriage and the comfortable integration of the social group into a renewed whole. That this book ends on a strong note of unresolved conflict suggests that a second book was already contemplated. (A promise of a second book is in fact given in a footnote to the last chapter.) Only at the conclusion of *Return* do we get the final resolution of the erotic conflict through the marriage of Tarzan and Jane, indeed in a double marriage, since Jane's friend Hazel married Lord Tennington. The society is whole, and, as usual in the healing of the comedic world, the misfit (Rokoff) is symbolically excluded from the new order in that "the French commander . . . gave immediate orders to place the Russian in irons and confine him on board the cruiser" (2.219).

But let us look a bit more closely at the conclusion of *Tarzan*, a veritable *tour de force* of erotic symbolism. The notion of passion as a fire is ancient, its origins lost in preliterature. The connection between flame and passion is well established in the earliest Greek literature, for the fire that destroys Troy is the fiery passion of Paris for Helen. The idea is developed extensively by the Roman poet Vergil in the second book of the *Aeneid*, and the Roman elegists work the metaphor of love and passion as consuming flame half to death.

The great fire in the Wisconsin forest to which Tarzan comes at the end of *Tarzan* is emblematic of the great erotic passions which, in their destructive ways, are raging in the two triangular relationships of Jane-Clayton-Canler and Jane-Clayton-Tarzan. As the forest fire seems at one point to burn out of control before being temporarily confined, so the passions directed to Jane as erotic heroine seem at several points to burn out of control and destroy her. The burning of the countryside is symbolic in the same sense that the burning of Troy is symbolic; human passions have overreached themselves and threaten to destroy or do destroy the society and social relationships that obtain in it.

Let us consider the first triangle. The expedition that brought the Porter group to Africa was for treasure (found but later "lost"), and it had been financed for Professor Porter by the villainous businessman Robert Canler. Canler's intent was more clearly erotic than commercial; his plan had been that when no treasure turned up, the professor's debt would be erased only if his daughter were given to him in marriage. Canler has now come to claim his payment.

Canler is merely the "civilized" analogue to Terkoz, for, although he does not abduct Jane by force and try to rape her, he is, as both he and Jane recognize and openly state, buying her (1.227f.) for the money lent to her father. After Canler's arrival, a dreadful "week passed" (1.229) during which hostilities smouldered and sparks of jealous rage flew among the unhappy group on the little farm. A fire has been burning for the whole week of impassioned suffering, and that very afternoon, in the east, it blazes out of control (1.230). Jane has wandered off into the woods "to be alone" and is trapped by the flames. Burroughs personifies the great fire as a villain whose erotic claims on Jane are about to destroy her. She makes desperate and futile attempts to get around the fire, but she discovers that the uncontrollable fire has

cut off her retreat as effectually as her advance had been cut off before.

A short run down the road brought her to a horrified stand, for there before her was another wall of flame. An arm of the main conflagration had shot out a half mile south of its parent to embrace this tiny strip of road in its implacable clutches. [1.232]

At this point in the unfolding erotic drama, Tarzan appears, takes control of the deteriorating situation, and sets off to search for Jane. It is implied that Clayton's wonted ineffectiveness is partially responsible for Jane's being trapped in the fire (1.232), which also makes metaphorical sense. As in the jungle, only Tarzan can effect a rescue. He finds Jane, and his rescue of her from the fire amounts to extricating her from the impossible dilemmas in which she has been placed. As the two of them walk back to the farm, the "wind had changed once more and the fire was burning back upon itself—another hour like that and it would be burned out" (1.233). Indeed, Tarzan's rescue of Jane from the burning fire is immediately paralleled by his rescue of her from marriage with the rapacious Canler. Canler's claims on Jane are dissolved by the letter of credit Tarzan gives to Professor Porter; Tarzan had found the lost treasure stolen by Porter's crew and had had it evaluated by experts.

Although Jane is technically free, she is indecisive about marrying Tarzan, as a result of her mental comparison of Tarzan with Clayton, the savage with the civilized (1.242). Although Jane does not marry Clayton in this book, she lets Tarzan understand he is next in line after Clayton. A sense of honor forces her to refuse Tarzan's suit, for a prior promise to Clayton must be kept. There is no question, however, whom she loves.

The tangled involvements with which the book ends are vividly—and scintillatingly—handled on the symbolic level by Burroughs in his exploitation of the fire. Since the resolution of one problem, the one with Canler, fails to solve anything but merely shifts the complications to the rivalry between Tarzan and Clayton, the underlying erotic discord is very much alive. Therefore, it is not irrelevant that they are all compelled to flee the Wisconsin countryside for town because the fire is after all *not* out, as Clayton reports (1.241). The fiery passions and erotic confusions are far from resolved, and on this point of emotional disequilibrium the novel ends.

The romantic triangle is picked up on the very second page (2.8) of *Return* and remains the consolidating motif holding that entire book together. Even such an apparently unrelated subnarrative as Tarzan's meeting with the Waziri and his elevation to their kingship has ultimate bearing on the amatory interests of the novel. In its indirect way, this story sets up Jane's final peril in Opar and her rescue by Tarzan from imminent death at La's sacrificing hand, a scene reminiscent of his rescue of Jane from the seemingly inescapable death by fire at the end of the first book. It is clear that Tarzan's thoughts remain on Jane (2.34), despite the many pleasurable distractions of Parisian life. It also becomes clear that Clayton begins rather early in the novel to assume some of the characteristics of the jilted Canler in *Tarzan*, for Clayton's increasing importunity in pressing for his and Jane's wedding recalls Canler's unpleasant exhortations.

After Burroughs has offered an unflattering comparison of Clayton's ineffectual efforts to rescue Jane, abducted by the Oparians, to Tarzan's purposeful mission (2.198–201), Clayton falls ill. He has already lost any real prospect of marrying Jane, and the fever, like the Wisconsin fire, becomes a symbolic device to underscore the point. The parching fever he suffers so dreadfully before finally dying serves the purely narrative end of eliminating Clayton and making it possible for Jane to marry Tarzan without having to break her word. Equally important, it also satisfies the symbolic requirement of the parallelism in the two erotic triangles, for the burning fever in the conclusion is thematically analogous to the burning fire in the previous novel. The distinction to be drawn is that the fire was emblematic of so consuming a passion that no erotic relationship could be consummated, but Clayton's fever is a personal passion so destructive that it eliminates the last rival and leaves no obstructions to the consummation of marriage between Jane and Tarzan.

The parallel love stories at the conclusion of the first and second novels should now be obvious. The procedure for presenting this erotic theme is Homeric in both conception and execution, for, as occurs so commonly in Homer, a given formulaic narrative in one place is repeated with slight changes (for example, in characters, scene, and vocabulary), at another point in the text *in order that each may comment on the other.* Neither is fully satisfactory by itself, but only as a unit do two or more thematically parallel passages "speak" to the reader, here in emphasizing an important aspect of the hero's growth and maturation.

The fairy tale structure in this heroic romance demands that the hero win his maiden only after overcoming obstacles, including repeated threats that someone else will marry his woman. The classical exemplar is, of course, Odysseus, who, again, is the one classical hero on whom Tarzan is most closely modeled. Odysseus, too, must eliminate Penelope's suitors before he can resume his role as husband and reestablish harmony in Ithaca. Jane's suitors have established a priamelistic (see Chapter 2 on the "priamel") hierarchy which places Tarzan at the pinnacle. First, the brute beast, Terkoz, wished to make Jane his wife (Tarzan kills him); next, the human rogue, Canler, wishes to marry Jane (Tarzan almost kills him); then, the infinitely superior Clayton wishes to have Jane to wife (Tarzan wanted to kill him at one point but ends up trying to save his life, in vain); and, finally, as the capping element of this extended priamel, Tarzan the hero marries the woman. The amatory romance fits neatly with the literary romance, or, as Burroughs self-consciously phrases it in the double-entendre on the last page: "And when they spoke of it (viz. the wedding) to the others they were assured that it would be quite regular, and a most splendid termination of a remarkable romance" (2.221).

This conclusion is thematically identical to that in *Son*, a novel in which the son's ontogeny is an obvious replication of paternal phylogeny. In *Son*, Meriem, who has been the object of much erotic attention by a number of males, both animal and human, is married to Korak. It turns out that Meriem is of noble lineage, or, as her father says, "She is a princess in her own right" (4.222). In this fairy tale with its strong elements of romance, it is appropriate that the hero should marry the princess at the end.

The ending of *Return* untangles the confusion found in the last pages of the previous novel, *Tarzan*, and destroys the powerful disequilibrium which it had created. We see that the repeated attacks on Jane should not, if we keep in mind the Homeric provenience of Burroughs' world, be construed as mindless repetition of a somehow "nasty" theme, but as a conventional iteration of a theme in a priamelistic structure for the purpose of enhancing the hero and magnifying his achievement once it is accomplished.

For Burroughs the idea of Darwinian evolution[4] is a central theme for validating his own position in the age-old controversy over the relative contribution of nature and nurture to the development of the individual. Unlike Rousseau and the romantic tradition of the Noble Savage, Burroughs most decidedly did not believe in the perfectibility of man. Although his Tarzan strikes an optimistic note about the possibilities for man, Burroughs does not favorably view humanity at large. There is too much of the beast in man, as Burroughs repeatedly reminds the reader.

In the novels of the half-century immediately preceding the beginning of Burroughs' writing in 1911, the theme of Darwinian evolution was exploited with great gusto and, to all appearances, to the increasing delight of growing audiences of readers.[5] Burroughs' Darwinism was part of the common literary property of the day. Hundreds, or perhaps even thousands, of these once fashionable writers are no longer remembered, but Burroughs has survived.

Although my primary concern has been the classical tradition in Burroughs' fiction, Darwinism is so pervasive in Burroughs that it cannot be ignored. Tarzan was the ideal vehicle for developing his thoughts on this subject, and as part of the thematic core of the Tarzan novels this modern theme has a counterpart in ancient literature and myth. Even though it would be misleading to suggest that Burroughs' use of the theme of Darwinism is based exclusively on classical authors and themes, it is a fact that evolution as such was a concept known to the Greeks.[6] It is related, moreover, in important ways to the adaptation of epic divine machinery in Burroughs' world. His extension of phylogeny to ontogeny allows him to elaborate on the relationship of the heroic protagonist not only to a modern version of ultimate ancestry (animals) but also to his most immediate ancestor, his father. This relationship is important to the definition of the classical hero. Each hero has a past and a future, a father and a son, and is himself both father and son; of the classical heroes, Vergil's Aeneas and Homer's Odysseus are the most relevant paradigms, each being defined as both father and son in his respective poem. This literary theme, then, with its modern designation of Darwinism, fits smoothly into the characterization of the heroes of ancient literature and myth that concerns itself with man's provenience.

Burroughs views Tarzan's personal growth and development as the recapitulation of human evolution in the form of a single individual. Tarzan is in effect turned into a paradigm for the human race and its laborious emergence from a state of dark ignorance and savagery to civilized status. Passage after passage addresses itself to this underlying analogy in Tarzan, and the description of his learning to read does so with special vividness: "Tarzan of the Apes, little primitive man, presented a picture filled, at once, with pathos and with promise—an allegorical figure of the primordial groping through the black night of ignorance toward the light of learning" (1.48). The tacit first premise in all of these passages is the understanding that the great apes among whom Tarzan has been reared are the forerunners of man. Early in *Tarzan*, this phylogenetic presupposition about the great apes is indicated in the auctorial commentary on the Dum-Dum, the ritual dance which the anthropoids celebrate on important tribal occasions.

From this primitive function has arisen, unquestionably, all the forms and ceremonials of modern church and state, for through all the countless ages, back beyond the uttermost ramparts of a dawning humanity our fierce, hairy forebears danced out the rites of the Dum-Dum to the sound of their earthen drums, beneath the bright light of a tropical moon in the depth of a mighty jungle which stands unchanged today as it stood on that long forgotten night in the dim, unthinkable vistas of the long dead past when our first shaggy ancestors swung from a swaying bough and dropped lightly upon the soft turf of the first meeting place [1.52].

The belief in evolutionary processes as guaranteeing the survival of the best and the fittest is voiced even before Tarzan himself appears on the scene, but one may well appreciate his own dedication to it in view of his father's thinking. When the Greystokes, parents of the yet unborn Tarzan, are abandoned in the jungle, Lord Greystoke attempts to comfort his wife by explaining that the two of them can recapitulate their phylogeny. They die, of course, but their son survives and exemplifies the principle that the father here enunciates: "Hundreds of thousands of years ago our ancestors of the dim and distant past faced the same problems which we must face in these same primeval forests. That we are here today evidences their victory" (1.16). The opening of the first novel gives an explicit statement about the evolutionary thread that is to run throughout the corpus. The idea that ontogeny recapitulates phylogeny in the case of Tarzan emerges explicitly in the passage in which Tarzan asks Jane to marry him (1.243). His journey is more one through evolutionary chronology than geographical distance, for in the brief period of his life he has compressed the development of the phylum from its primitive ancestors to the modern British aristocracy. Ontogeny repeats phylogeny.

Burroughs' evolutionary themes do not promote the straightforward and simplistic celebration of man as king of creation, the be-all and end-all of eons of developmental trends, despite the unfortunate and reductive interpretations of some hostile critics. Thus, from the description of the Dum-Dum as the precursor of modern rituals and institutions, Brian V. Street generalizes, quite unfairly, about Burroughs' "belief in progress,"[7] but he never discusses any of those passages in which the author's evolutionary theme is played in reverse, as it were. The anti-evolutionism of Opar, for example (2.172–173), is representative of Burroughs' larger concern in this area. Physical evolution towards a "better" appearance is not necessarily the same as evolution in the moral or ethical sphere (see, for example, 2.17). At the same time that it corrupts, as it corrupts Tarzan by instilling in him avarice for gold (see 2.128, 2.160), civilization also inculcates values that most would consider good, as it teaches Tarzan that murder is no solution (see 2.125).

The anti-evolutionary thread that runs through the novels is especially prominent in *Son*. Here the apeman's boy, Jack, alias Korak, unlearns much of what he has been taught during the first years of his life in civilized society, including many ingenuous ideas about his fellow man. The narrative is so presented that the reader cannot fail to appreciate Burroughs' strong criticism of one type of education and equally strong endorsement of another kind. Jack must begin anew, as an ape (that is, as Korak), tutored by the ape Akut and not Mr. Moore, "the bilious-countenances, studious young man" (4.13), and so recapitulate the experience of his father. Jack must retrogress in order to progress; the potential is in him, but it can only be brought out by the savage jungle.

There is more to this theme in Burroughs than meets the uncritical eye. Any devil can quote scripture to suit his own purpose. It is true that Burroughs generally considered Tarzan as the superb result of generations of evolutionary development, but it is inaccurate to suggest that Burroughs therefore viewed modern man and the world of his day as the ultimate achievement of evolution. The sustained synkrisis between the London Greystokes and Tarzan, for example, reveals the fallibility of simplistic equations in these matters. Much of Burroughs' writing (Tarzan, as well as the anti-worlds of his science fiction and Westerns) is bitingly satirical and critical of the depths to which the contemporary world has sunk. The theme of evolutionary Darwinism in Burroughs entails certain ambiguities.

A similar ambiguity inheres in the closely allied theme of external appearance versus inner reality. If evolutionary progress is measurable by external criteria, and if some criteria are agreed or assumed to be superior to others, then it is an easy matter to propose a hierarchical structure that encompasses best and worst on a defined scale. The reductive view would have us believe, for example, that in Burroughs all animals are, on the evolutionary scale, inferior to all men, all blacks are inferior to all whites, all forms of religion are expressions of primitive superstition, and so forth. Support for these views can be gleaned by a selective culling of Burroughs' texts, but the distortions will remain. Some animals are presented as inferior to humans (for example, Terkoz to Jane); some blacks are inferior to whites (for example, the blacks of Mbonga's village); and some religious practices are seen as primitive superstition even by the practicing believer (for example, Momaya's critique of Bukawai at 6.93). But it is equally true that some animals are superior to humans (for example, the ape Akut to Paulvitch in *Beasts*); some blacks are superior to whites (for example, Mugambi to Werper in *Jewels*); and some religious forms are based not on superstition but on reasoned speculation (for example, Tarzan's growing sense of "god" in *Tales*). Again, the overwhelming desire to find proof in Burroughs' novels that he was a simple-minded hack who could neither write nor think leads to misrepresentations. Burroughs' evolutionary branches do not always grow straight and uninterrupted, and the facts are somewhat more complicated than is often represented.

Unfortunately, the external appearance is not always a reliable index to the inner reality. We already know that the glitter of civilization often comes from tinsel, and we also know that the murky dark of the vine-covered jungle can be a place of refuge and calm. One might think that all physically ugly beings are, like the Oparians, morally ugly as well. This is often the case, but it is not an invariable rule. A striking exception is the "uncouth" and "unsavory cook" on the ship *Kincaid* in *Beasts*. The description of this repulsive Swede is compelling.

The man was tall and raw-boned, with a long yellow moustache, an unwholesome complexion, and filthy nails. The very sight of him with one grimy thumb buried deep in the lukewarm stew, that seemed, from the frequency of its repetition, to constitute the pride of his culinary art, was sufficient to take away the girl's appetite.

His small, blue, close-set eyes never met hers squarely. There was a shiftiness of his whole appearance that even found expression in the cat-like manner of his gait, and to it all a sinister suggestion was added by the long slim knife that always rested at his waist, slipped through the greasy cord that supported his soiled apron [3.16].

This introduction to Anderssen sets him up as a villain, for he has all the external characteristics of the moral degenerate: physical ugliness, dirtiness, sloppiness, and a sinister animality. He has apparently never quite evolved into a civilized human being but is still in the bestial range of the evolutionary scale. That he is not what he seems to be becomes clear a few pages later when we learn that he will help Jane escape from Rokoff and in the event proves himself her courageous and resolute defender. She eventually realizes that the cook with his bestial appearance is infinitely superior to the supposedly civilized scoundrel Rokoff who is trying to use her for his nefarious purposes. Appearances are truly deceiving (3.74, 3.91). The characterization of Anderssen suggests that there is more than one way to view the evolutionary theme in Burroughs. Again, it is not a question of evolution always and automatically tending toward the *summum bonum* of British aristocratic man, for in the case of Anderssen the moral *summum*, equally the result of evolutionary tendencies, is discovered in a deformed commoner.

Another example of this reverse Darwinian theme involves the British aristocrat, the Honorable Morison Baynes, whose role in *Son* begins as a kind of inversion of Anderssen's and finally concludes in the same vein as his. As first introduced to us, Baynes is an effete lover of luxury who embodies the Victorian interpretation of Darwinism as inevitably creating in the British aristocracy of the period its crowning achievement. Baynes finds "all things un-European as rather more than less impossible" (4.130), and he entertains hypocritical views about "those he considered of meaner clay" (4.130). However, moral corruption bred into him is masked by a deceptively handsome exterior (4.130). His designs on Meriem are decidedly dishonorable; to him she is an amusing diversion. But after various complications and cliff-hanging twists in the plot, Meriem is abducted by an evil Swede whose intentions are at least as dishonorable as those of Baynes. A moral metamorphosis takes place in Baynes. Love transforms wickedness into goodness (the theme is common in Burroughs), ennobles the vilest of intentions, and launches the erstwhile cad on a mission of mercy to rescue Meriem from Swedish abuse. As Baynes' ethics change, his external appearance also begins to alter markedly. Where a former nastiness was wrapped in external finery, the burgeoning sense of probity goes dressed in rags and physical disfigurement (4.179). The change of opprobrious behavior into noble self-sacrifice through the transforming agency of love for a woman may seem a dated notion for the modern reader, but it is one point of view about the relationship between a man and a woman. One cannot deny that it is an idea and that the author is making a point. Eager to show that Burroughs was without any meaning at all, one critic claims that his work "didn't mean a thing and you couldn't make it mean a thing if you tried."[8] This assessment is transparent nonsense, and in this particular case it obscures the connection of the idea of a transmuting love to the larger theme of moral evolutionism that it exemplifies.

The theme that the exterior is not a reliable indicator of the inner reality is conceptually linked with the larger theme of Darwinism. Tarzan is the most conspicuous exemplification of this relationship between the themes, but both Anderssen and Baynes also illustrate the point. Baynes, the pinnacle of phylogenetic evolution, is a moral brute; Anderssen, an evolutionary disaster in appearance, represents the pinnacle of moral evolution. At the same time, Baynes' brutishness is transformed, and the transformation is reflected in the misleadingly ugly exterior; Anderssen's ugliness has become a kind of beauty in Jane's eyes. In the series of transformations involving Tarzan and Anderssen (3.79–82), a clear connection is made between Tarzan's beastliness and reversion to beastness on the one hand, and between his change back to humanness and simultaneous humaneness on the other hand. The physical change from beastness to humanness is paralleled in the moral transformation from beastliness to humaneness.[9] This ontogenetic recapitulation of phylogenetic evolution is a paradigm for moral evolution. To become a human being presumably entails a dawning of moral awareness.

In other passages in which the Darwinian theme is presented, physical primitivism is seen to hide a moral superiority. The animal point of view recommends itself over the so-called civilized one. Here Burroughs makes a distinction between physical and moral Darwinism, asserting that the more developed on the evolutionary scale an individual or a society is, the more primitive it is in dealing with itself. The problem gets to the very core of Tarzan's mediating function as hero in the novels, for he is always trying to resolve this apparently irreconcilable contradiction in his mind or in his actions. Will becoming civilized make him a better, a more moral person? It would be comforting to answer an unequivocal yes or no, but Burroughs' exploration of the problem does not admit of a simple reply. In a sense civilization does civilize, and men's spiritual or moral evolution is in harmony with his physical evolution. It is also true that civilization brutalizes and emphasizes the vast gulf between man's apparently (that is, externally visible) advanced stage of evolutionary development and the truly (that is, internally real) primitive moral sensibility he displays. The corollary of this thesis is that the relatively unadvanced animals of the jungle carry within themselves an innately superior knowledge of what, in Burroughs' world, constitutes moral probity. The ambiguous point is that sometimes the external indices of the most advanced evolutionary development are in fact true indices of the interior reality, but at other times the externals, whether they indicate virtue or depravity, are quite deceptive.

Although both his father and mother die early in the first novel, Tarzan feels the influence of his father for a long time. His father is somehow still present for Tarzan, his ideals vivid and his aristocratic bequest still being paid out. The son is constantly seen against the background of paternal ancestry, and not a little of our understanding of Tarzan derives from our acquaintance with the father. This tight and inseparable link between the two is an extension of the Darwinian theme that permeates the novels. It does for the personal ancestry and personal inheritance of Tarzan what the theme of evolution does for Tarzan as heroic emblem of both mankind and everyman. Tarzan's father, it will be recalled, is intensely conscious that he belongs to an ancient tradition that extends to the beginnings of mankind (see 1.16f.). It is a catholic perspective of self in relation to the past, an awareness of ultimate provenience. The ontogenetic heritage on which Tarzan is drawing has itself been tied to phylogeny.

This link between past and present, that sense of personal continuity from father to son which is so obsessive a theme in ancient literature, is of fundamental importance in Burroughs. His hero belongs within a larger network of both temporal and social relationships. The father guarantees the legitimacy of the hero's ontogeny, and for that reason he hovers constantly in the background. To the casual reader these references to the dead father may seem irrelevant or, worse, mere formulaic filler, but one must recognize that in the tradition in which Burroughs is creating his hero, the father in a sense never dies. Even if he is physically dead, his ideals are not.

Burroughs' thoroughgoing Darwinism offers a remarkably consistent analogue to the concept of divine genealogy in ancient literature. The underlying dynamics in each case are identical—namely, the desire to connect the present to the past and so to see the present as part of an ongoing continuum—but the specific formulation differs in each case.

Whereas the Greek view of human origins insists constantly and continually on the gods, the Darwinian thesis insists with equal firmness on animals, especially on the great apes who reared Tarzan. Burroughs is consistent in his adaptation of the divine machinery of antiquity to the world of Tarzan, for his emphatic Darwinism can be seen as the modern equivalent of the ancient conviction that the gods, not animals, will be found at the source. The two approaches are in one sense identical and in another, diametrically opposed. Divine origins begin on high and move down to man; animal origins start at the bottom and move up to man. It may be noted that while mythological stemmata invariably place the gods at the top and then descend to the hero in question, the Darwinian "tree" places the animals lower on the structure and man in the uppermost branches.

The grand adaptation which the emphasis on Darwinism represents once more underscores the thoroughly traditional cast of Burroughs' novels. At the same time, it calls attention to his powerful capacity for invention, for what Burroughs has done is intrinsic to the tradition in which his novels are conceived; yet, it is a modern update of a fundamental and perennial question: where do we come from?

The Greek view does not necessarily imply a more exalted attitude towards man than Burroughs'. The divinities from whom the heroes sprang were often riddled with the worst human defects and vices, and often the animals of Burroughs are imbued with the finest and most noble of human sentiments. Both outlooks are basically pessimistic about man in the aggregate, but they are equally hopeful about the exceptional individual, the hero, who is in touch with both his phylogenetic and his ontogenetic past.

Analogies may crumble if pressed too hard, but the parallel between Greek divine descent and Darwinian descent of the heroic type is greatly strengthened by the unspoken givens in each case. Although Burroughs' Darwinian tracing of Tarzan's heroic origins never goes beyond the anthropoid "ancestors" of mankind, Darwinian theory itself takes the provenience infinitely further. Going sufficiently far into the past would take us to the very origins of life and even the universe, but nothing is ever hinted or even suggested about this antecedent span in the first six Tarzan novels. We do know, however, that the concept of the earlier period of evolution that would involve us in palaeontological and geological scales of time was neither unknown nor untreated by Burroughs in other books, most notably *The Land That Time Forgot* (published in 1924).

A similar situation exists with the Greek material. Although purely heroic genealogies never concern themselves with the generations that came before those of the hero's ancestral gods such as Zeus or Poseidon, it was, of course, general knowledge that neither the world nor the gods began with Zeus and his contemporaries. The tacit but well-known assumption behind Zeus was the story of the creation from the beginnings of time. This account is most completely familiar to us from the version that the early poet Hesiod, a contemporary of Homer, records in his *Theogony*, or *Origins of the Gods*, probably sometime in the late eighth century B.C. Here we learn first of the creation of gods and finally of the coming of Zeus and his brethren who engage in a struggle of Darwinian dimensions to determine the ultimate ruler of the Greek pantheon. Although these pre-Jovian generations are of little, if any, consequence in the establishment of heroic genealogies, they are a fixed part of the tradition about the gods and appear in many other contexts throughout ancient literature. Burroughs' Darwinism, then, fits in a very fundamental sense into the larger tradition of classical heroic literature on which he is constantly drawing.

Another theme merits comment, that is, the relationship between parent and child. It manifests itself as father-son, mother-son, and father-daughter but, curiously enough, rarely as mother-daughter. Even the most elementary acquaintance with classical myth will show that the theme of parent-child is everywhere.

The frequency with which father and son are brought into contact with each other in myth is reflected in the commonness of this theme in ancient literature. The sense of the son's obligations to the father and the father's line is overpowering in the *Iliad*. Indeed, it is often seen as an oppressive hold that the paternal past exercises on the present. The *Odyssey* pursues the parallel developments of father and son and brings the two together at the end of the poem. Nor do we lack in the many heroic biographies the close ties between a mother and her son.

The ancient material depicts both parents and children as mentally hostile to each other but also as offering mutual support. For example, father Anchises helps his son Aeneas at every turn, but father Tantalus is outrageously cruel to his son Pelops; son Hermes can be very helpful to his father Zeus, but son Oedipus kills his father Laius; mother Thetis helps her son Achilles win glory, but mother Althea is implacable to her son Meleager; son Kronos helps his mother Gaia, but son Orestes kills his mother Clytemnestra; father Danaus supports his daughters, the Danaids, but father Agamemnon sacrifices his daughter Iphigeneia; and, finally, daughter Antigone stands by her father Oedipus, but daughter Scylla behaves savagely to her father Nisus.

What has all of this to do with Burroughs? Burroughs displays here, as elsewhere, his indebtedness to ancient literature, for he uses the basic relationship between parent and child as a common theme for characterization.

Tarzan's connection with his adoptive mother is instructive, for it reveals the traditionality of Tarzan's heroic role. Like both Achilles with his divine mother Thetis and Odysseus with the ghost (that is, otherworldly) of his mother Anticleia, for example, Tarzan is aided at every step by his mother Kala. Although the foundling she rears does not develop as the other children of the tribe, Kala insists on keeping it and looking out for its interests. When Tarzan is in danger, Kala is the first on hand to aid him (1.38, 1.45), and when he has been seriously wounded in his battle with Bolgani the gorilla, only Kala's solicitous attentions during his convalescence ensure his survival (1.46). Only when Tarzan has reached maturity and can stand alone does Kala die. No divine mother from Homer or Vergil ever displayed more concern for her male offspring than Kala did for her Tarzan. By and large, the great heroes of ancient literature have mothers who favor and support them, and Tarzan is part of that tradition.

Tarzan's relationship to his foster father, Tublat, is an entirely different matter. Kala's cranky mate is constantly trying to harm or even kill Tarzan, and during Tarzan's youth only Kala's faithful vigilance prevents his undoing (1.34). This little triangular drama involving an alliance of mother and son against the father comes straight out of heroic legend and divine myth. The narratives that deal with the Greek foundations of the universe and the origins of the gods are based, as doublets, on this archetypal pattern. As Hesiod tells the story in his *Theogony*, first mother Gaia (Earth) prevails on her youngest son Kronos to help her against the savagery of her mate Ouranos (Heaven). Kronos, doing his duty by his mother, deposes his father Ouranos by killing him. In the next generation the story repeats itself, for now Kronos has become high-minded and insolent in his behavior to wife and children. Mother Rhea therefore takes as ally her son Zeus against the tyrannical father Kronos, and Zeus deposes him. These deposing sons in the myths become rulers or kings of their contemporaries, and not long after Tarzan has slain Tublat, his father, he also slays Kerchak, the king of the tribe, and himself becomes king.

The occasion for Tarzan's patricide follows the identical pattern of the ancient myths. Gaia wants to do something about her husband because he is physically abusing her, and Rhea suffers psychological torture from her husband's peculiar habit of swallowing each child as it is born. In each case, the son steps into the breach to save the mother-wife from the outrages of the father-husband. In the death of Tublat an identical cause is to be seen. Tublat has gone mad with rage at Tarzan, and the only available object on which to express his anger is the unfortunate Kala who had not been quick enough to escape his rampage. The parent-child relationship in this minidrama is too thoroughly mythic in its configuration to have been the result of inadvertence on Burroughs' part.

The relationships Kala-Tarzan and Tublat-Tarzan are not the only examples of mother-son and father-son patterns in the works of Burroughs. Although only briefly alluded to, Tarzan's real mother also belongs here, for she too, as long as she lived, was in all respects, save that of her mental confusion, a devoted and supportive mother of her infant (1.24). In *Tales* the same basic pattern is clear in the relationship between the young black boy Tibo, whom Tarzan wishes to adopt, and Tibo's mother, Momaya. Indeed, the woman's very name, *Momaya*,[10] indicates where the emphasis is being placed in this narrative. Tarzan functions as a kind of supposititious father in this triangle, as a foundling father, so to speak, who tries to but soon realizes he cannot be a father by force. At any rate Momaya displays the characteristic behavior of other mothers in the novels in that she is fearful for her son's safety and protective to a degree that transcends reason (6.70), willing to go to any length to restore her son (6.76), and without restraint in avenging the fraudulent help the witch doctor has given her (6.104).

The same pattern is found in the role mother Teeka and son Gazan play opposite each other. Teeka is fiercely protective of her newborn son (6.37f.), and when he is in trouble she behaves in a fashion that for the apes can only be deemed irrational. Despite her enormous dread of snakes, she has no hesitation about hurling herself into combat with a reptile in order to rescue her infant (6.61). When Teeka becomes the object of Toog's sexual attentions, the rogue ape is able to capture Teeka only by threatening her child in such a way that she abandons caution for herself to save her son (6.144f.).

Tarzan's wife, Jane, is of course also a mother, and in both *Beasts* and *Son* her relationship to Jack (Korak) is portrayed in most vivid terms. In *Beasts* the infant son has been kidnapped, and the mother permits herself to clutch at straws and undertake a most foolish enterprise in an attempt to regain the child and save it from death. In this regard she is no different from Kala, Momaya, or Teeka. Again, in *Son*, her fear and worry over her lost son is true to the general pattern. All of these mothers wish desperately to help their offspring, and although they are not always successful immediately, in the final analysis each sees her son restored to her through her own courage, persistence, cleverness, or combination thereof.

This ancient mythic pattern of the relationship between a mother and her son quite generally interested Burroughs. With the other parent-child relationships, it suggests that Burroughs, like the ancients, had strong convictions about the integrity of the family as a unit of social life, be it of the white world, the black world, or the animal world. Since we have few details about Burroughs' own relationship to his parents, any speculation about his varying affections for his mother and his father must be deemed risky.[11] While personal reasons may be responsible for Burroughs' treatment of these mother-son relationships and the difficulties in family constellations, we can assume that here we are dealing more with matters of traditional depictions of the hero than with autobiographical elements. Ultimate truth in the question is perhaps unobtainable.

The widely dispersed theme of parent-child serves the important end of insisting on the value of the family in society. When the family is in order, the world is in order and makes sense; when the family is split and relationships are not clear, the world itself is disjointed. This idea, though, is not original with Burroughs. In adapting it, Burroughs once more insists on Tarzan as the traditional hero in a recognizable milieu of traditional themes. Among these themes, in addition to those treated above, are those of beauty and the beast, burials, clothing, disguises, disease and wounds, food and eating, hunting, capture and imprisonment, escape, shipwreck, rebirth, ransom, treasure, love triangles, marriage, and identity and heritage.

CONCLUSION

One reason why the *Iliad* and the *Odyssey* have survived is that even today they say something to contemporary man about his aspirations and his dealings with himself and the world. The *Odyssey* is largely "fairy tale" and improbable coincidence; nonetheless, the *Odyssey* continues to be read, pondered, and enjoyed. Every person can see himself in Odysseus; every person undertakes his own odyssey. The escapist fantasy that permeates so much of the *Odyssey* takes us out of ourselves and into those fairylands where we can master our surroundings, control our own destinies, and be what we cannot always be in the real world we inhabit. Fantasy and escape in literature exorcise our innermost demons and allow us to function in the diurnal world; fantasy has always engaged us, from the first story read to us to the latest escapist fare we have come across.

Edgar Rice Burroughs is a writer in the Homeric mold. He evokes those deep yearnings for adventure, risk, power, romance, and self-control that most human beings have but perhaps do not admit to. The appeal of Tarzan is as immediate as the appeal of the Homeric Odysseus, and those readers of Tarzan who like Tarzan will love the *Odyssey*, as well as much else in classical literature. The violence, cruelty, inconsistency, escapism, law-and-order advocacy, romance, otherworldly intervention, improbability, and so forth that are so roundly condemned and vilified in the Tarzan stories trace their ancestry to the universally praised tale of Odysseus. For Burroughs, as we have seen, was familiar with the ancient languages themselves. Burroughs' language is strongly reminiscent of the language and style of Greek and Latin. In his much-maligned repetition of language, motifs, and themes, we see a clear analogue to the organic wholeness of Homeric epic, and his alleged stylistic defectiveness in fact constitutes the very bedrock on which his heroic fantasy is constructed. The techniques and materials on which he constantly relies have been seen to derive largely from the antecedents of classical prototypes: the parallel plot, thematic multiplication, ring composition, heroic pattern, polarity, mythos, synkrisis, chiasmus, divine machinery, and a host of others. Burroughs, like all good traditionalists, was able to use his antecedents without mindless imitation; he remained firmly rooted in a past tradition and at the same time was an inventive innovator on its patterns. Whatever its sources in shared conventions of form or collective memory of theme, the power that makes us respond to the wanderings of Odysseus is also at work in Burroughs' Tarzan, and the two great popular heroes speak openly to our most cherished fantasies.

Appendix I

────────────TWO FORMULAIC PASSAGES

Consider a detailed analysis of one sequence in Burroughs (Tarzan giving utterance to his victory cry after slaying a lion) and one in Homer (the killing of a warrior on the battlefield). We begin with the sequence in Burroughs.

1. As the body rolled to the ground Tarzan of the Apes placed his foot under the neck of his lifelong enemy and, raising his eyes to the full moon, threw back his fierce young head and voiced the wild and terrible cry of his people (1.56).

2. Then the strange figure which had vanquished it (viz. a lion) stood erect upon the carcass, and throwing back the wild and handsome head, gave out the fearsome cry . . . (1.113).

3. Then with his foot upon the carcass of Numa, he raised his voice in the awesome victory cry of his savage tribe (1.219).

4. . . . he leaped upon the mighty carcass, and gave voice to the weird challenge with which he announced a great victory (2.133).

5. . . . leap to his feet beside the corpse of his foe, and placing one foot upon the broken neck lift his voice in the hideous challenge of the victorious bull-ape (3.80).

6. . . . rise from the vanquished foe, and placing a foot upon the still quivering carcass, raise his face to the moon and bay out a hideous cry (5.20).

7. The ape-man placed a foot upon her [zebra's] carcass and raised his voice in the victory call of the Mangani [i.e., great apes] (5.60).

8. He placed a foot upon the dead body of the panther, and lifting his blood-stained face to the blue of the equatorial heavens, gave voice to the horrid victory cry of the bull ape (6.47).

9. He placed a foot upon the prostrate form and raising his face to the heavens gave voice to the kill cry of the bull ape (6.141).

As in all the other set passages in Burroughs, this set contains its formulas of motif and language. The obvious components are the following.

A. the body of the victim
B. Tarzan's foot on (part of) the body
C. Tarzan raises eyes/head
D. the cry

The particulars may also be noted.

A. 1. as the body rolled to the ground
   2. carcass
   3. carcass of Numa
   4. the mighty carcass
   5. the corpse of his foe
   6. still quivering carcass
   7. her [zebra's] carcass
   8. the dead body of the panther
   9. prostrate form

B. 1. Tarzan of the Apes placed his foot upon the neck
   2. stood erect upon
   3. with his foot upon
   4. leaped upon
   5. placing one foot upon the broken neck
   6. placing a foot upon
   7. placed a foot upon
   8. placed a foot upon
   9. placed a foot upon

C. 1. raising his eyes to the full moon, threw back his fierce young head
   2. throwing back the wild and handsome head

3. BLANK
4. BLANK
5. BLANK
6. raise his face to the moon
7. BLANK
8. lifting his blood-stained face to the blue of the equatorial heavens
9. raising his face to the heavens

D. 1. voiced the wild and terrible cry of his people
3. gave out the fearsome cry
3. raised his voice in the awesome victory cry of his savage tribe
4. gave voice to the weird challenge with which he announced a great victory
5. lift his voice in the hideous challenge of the victorious bull-ape
6. bay out a hideous cry
7. raised his voice in the victory call of the Mangani
8. gave voice to the horrid victory cry of the bull ape
9. gave voice to the kill cry of the bull ape

The verbal and motival formulas come thick and fast, in predictable sequence. These passages from Burroughs are analogous in execution and design to many types of formulaic scenes in Homeric poetry. Homer's general practice is readily suggested by a presentation of some examples that describe the dying of men on the battlefield.

1. . . . in his [Echepolus'] forehead the bronze spear point stuck and crossed through the bone inside; darkness covered his two eyes, and he tumbled. . . (*Iliad* 4.460–462).

2. . . . in the side of the forehead; . . . the bronze spear crossed right through the other temple; darkness covered his two eyes, and he fell loudly (*Iliad* 4.502–504).

3. . . . and Hector stuck the spear-shaft in his chest, and in the presence of his dear friends he killed him. . . (*Iliad* 15.650–651).

4. Agamemnon stuck the spear-shaft in the back between the shoulders of his first man after he had turned, and he drove it right on through the chest, and the man fell loudly. . . (*Iliad* 5.40–42).

5. . . . Diomedes stuck the spear-shaft in the back between the

shoulders of the man after he had turned around, and drove it right on through the chest, and the man tumbled from his chariot (*Iliad* 8.258–260).

6. . . . [Antilochus] chanced to pierce his midsection with the spear-shaft, and the bronze breastplate which he was wearing did not hold. But it stuck in the middle of his belly, and he fell gasping out of the well-wrought chariot (*Iliad* 13.397–399).

7. . . . [Ajax] undid his [Cleoboulus'] strength with a stroke of the hilted sword to his neck. The sword got warm all over from the blood; but his [Cleoboulus'] two eyes a ruddy death and resistless fate took fast hold of (*Iliad* 16.332–334).

8. . . . [Achilles] drove with his hilted sword down the middle of Echeclus' head. The sword got warm all over from the blood: but his two eyes a ruddy death and resistless fate took fast hold of (*Iliad* 20. 475–477).

9. . . . [Diomedes] drove at the middle of his [Dolon's] neck with his blade and cut off both tendons. The head of the man, trying to speak, mingled with the dust (*Iliad* 10.455–457).

The generalized formula consists of these elements.

A. part of the body wounded
B. weapons used
C. weapon's action
D. the death itself
E. the dead man's fall
F. ornamentation

The specifics should also be observed.

A. 1. forehead
2. side of the forehead
3. chest
4. in the back between the shoulders
5. in the back between the shoulders
6. midsection, middle of the belly
7. neck

8. middle of the head
9. middle of the neck

B. 1. bronze spear point
2. bronze spear point
3. spear-shaft
4. spear-shaft
5. spear-shaft
6. spear-shaft
7. stroke of hilted sword
8. hilted sword
9. dash of blade

C. 1. stuck and crossed through the bone
2. crossed right through the other temple
3. stuck
4. stuck . . . drove it right on through the chest
5. stuck . . . drove it right on through the chest
6. pierce . . . stuck
7. BLANK
8. drove down
9. drove . . . cut off both tendons

D. 1. darkness covered his two eyes
2. darkness covered his two eyes
3. killed him
4. BLANK
5. BLANK
6. BLANK
7. his two eyes a ruddy death and resistless fate took fast hold of
8. his two eyes a ruddy death and resistless fate took fast hold of
9. BLANK

E. 1. he tumbled
2. he fell loudly
3. BLANK
4. he fell loudly
5. the man tumbled from his chariot
6. he fell gasping out of the well-wrought chariot
7. BLANK
8. BLANK
9. the head of the man, trying to speak, mingled with the dust

F. 1. BLANK
    2. BLANK
    3. BLANK
    4. after he had turned
    5. after he had turned
    6. the bronze breastplate which he was wearing did not hold
    7. the sword got warm all over from the blood
    8. the sword got warm all over from the blood
    9. BLANK

There is no need to go into the technical details of Homeric metrics and the metrical and linguistic exigencies that shaped these features of verbal repetition, but it must be understood that there are perhaps hundreds of such formulaic sequences in both Homer and Burroughs. Some of these, like battle-deaths in Homer and Tarzan's victory-cry in Burroughs, seem to be almost exclusively denotative; others, like those dealing with the jungle in Burroughs, are developed into major symbols.

Appendix II
GENEALOGY OF TARZAN OF THE APES, LORD GREYSTOKE

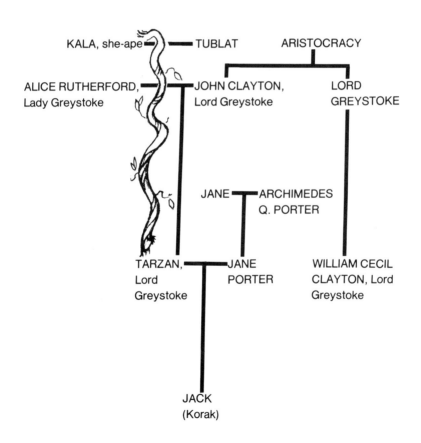

KALA, she-ape — TUBLAT   ARISTOCRACY

ALICE RUTHERFORD, — JOHN CLAYTON,   LORD
Lady Greystoke   Lord Greystoke   GREYSTOKE

JANE — ARCHIMEDES
Q. PORTER

TARZAN, — JANE   WILLIAM CECIL
Lord   PORTER   CLAYTON, Lord
Greystoke   Greystoke

JACK
(Korak)

Appendix III
TYPICAL ELEMENTS
OF HEROIC BIOGRAPHY

1. The hero's mother is a royal virgin.
2. His father is a king, and
3. Often a near relative of his mother, but
4. The circumstances of his conception are unusual, and
5. He is also reputed to be the son of a god.
6. At birth an attempt is made, usually by his father or maternal grandfather, to kill him, but
7. He is spirited away and
8. Reared by foster parents in a far country.
9. We are told nothing of his childhood, but
10. On reaching manhood he returns or goes to his future kingdom.
11. After a victory over the king and/or a giant, dragon, or wild beast,
12. He marries a princess, often the daughter of his predecessor, and
13. Becomes king.
14. For a time he reigns uneventfully, and
15. Prescribes laws, but
16. Later he loses favor with the gods and/or subjects, and
17. Is driven from the throne and city, after which
18. He meets with a mysterious death,
19. Often at the top of a hill.
20. His children, if any, do not succeed him.
21. His body is not buried, but nevertheless
22. He has one or more holy sepulchres.

Source: Adapted from Fitzroy Richard Somerset, Lord Raglan, *The Hero: A Study in Tradition, Myth, and Drama* (New York: Vantage Books Inc., 1956).

NOTES

Introduction

1. Francis Birrell, "The Glories of Excess," *The New Statesman and Nation* 3 (21 May 1932): 661f.

2. Edward T. Ewen, "Eh-wa-au-wau-aooow," *New York Times*, 23 September 1962: 157.

3. George P. Elliott, "Getting Away from the Chickens," *Hudson Review* 12 (Fall 1959): 395. Gore Vidal, "Tarzan Revisited," *Esquire* 60 (December 1963): 262.

4. *Nation* 102 (6 April 1916): 386.

5. *Boston Transcript* for 14 September 1920. *Independent* 82 (19 April 1915): 121.

6. Rudolph Altrocchi, *Sleuthing in the Stacks* (Cambridge, Mass.: Harvard University Press, 1944), p. 90.

7. Kingsley Amis, *New Maps of Hell: A Survey of Science Fiction* (New York: Harcourt, Brace, 1960), p. 454.

8. E. H. Lacon-Watson, "'Tarzan' and Literature," *Fortnightly* 119 (23 June 1923): 1044.

9. *The Fantastic in Literature* (Princeton, N.J.: University of Princeton Press, 1976), p. 4.

10. Brian V. Street, *The Savage in Literature: Representations of 'Primitive' Society in English Fiction 1858–1920* (London: Routledge & K. Paul, 1975), *passim*. Henrik Levinsen, " 'Vildmanden Tarzan' af Edgar R. Burroughs," *Børne og ungdomsbøger: Problemer og analyser* (Copenhagen: Gyldendal, 1969), pp. 140f., edited by Sven M. Kristensen and Preben Ramløv.

The objection might be raised that any child marooned as Tarzan was could never have learned to speak and would in fact have become autistic. A psychiatrist is cited by Paul Mandel, "Tarzan and the Paperbacks," *Life* (29

November 1963): 11, as feeling "that there is something sick about Tarzan's return" because he appeals to "our primitive instincts." Is the *Odyssey* sick, too?

11. Street, *The Savage in Literature*, p. 77.

12. *Nation* 102 (6 April 1916): 386.

13. As the Nazis did, because both books and films contained "undesirable elements" and offended "Nazi principles of race-consciousness" as well as those of "matrimony and womanly dignity." (See Robert W. Fenton, *The Big Swingers* [Englewood Cliffs, N.J.: Prentice-Hall, 1967] pp. 102f). But Burroughs was in good company: on the evening of 10 May 1933, he went up in the same flames that consumed Einstein, Mann, Freud, and Zola.

14. For his reliance of formulas, see John Seeyle in his review of Irwin Porges' biography of Burroughs, *New York Times Book Review* 80 (26 October 1975): 38; for belief in Darwinian evolution, see *Springfield Republican* for 17 August 1924, p. 7A, in a review of *The Land That Time Forgot*; for inferiority to Kipling, see *Boston Transcript* for 14 September 1920, p. 7, in a review of *Tarzan the Untamed*; for preposterousness, see Mandel, "Tarzan and the Paperbacks"; for antireligious tendencies and right-wing extremism, see John T. Flautz, "An American Demagogue in Barsoom," *Journal of Popular Culture* 1 (1967): 264, 271; for excessive violence, see Levinsen, "'Vildmanden Tarzan'"; and for infantile appeal, see Eike Barmeyer, *Science-Fiction: Theorie und Geschichte* (Munich: W. Fink, 1972). His condescending dismissal (p. 97) coyly suggests that Burroughs' books may "ganz nützliche Unterhaltungslektüre für Halbwüchsige sein" (be rather useful literature as diversion for the half-grown).

15. Truly remarkable in its twisting of logic is the comment by Roger Lancelyn Green, *Into Other Worlds, Space-Flight in Fiction, from Lucian to Lewis* (London: Abelard Schuman, 1958), who says that Burroughs' books have a "truly amazing power of invention which can stimulate the imagination, *though he had little of that deeper quality himself*" (p. 129; italics added).

16. Elliott, "Getting Away from the Chickens."

17. "ERB and the Heroic Epic," *Riverside Quarterly* 3 (March 1968): 122. This little paper is among the best of the serious criticism on Burroughs, and although I cannot accept some of his comments (as on the *deus ex machina*), he is correct in seeing the direct link between classical literature and Burroughs' world. One only wishes that he had pursued his ideas more thoroughly.

18. Dorothy McGreal, "The Burroughs No One Knows," *The World of Comic Art* 1.2 (Fall 1966): 15.

19. Richard Kyle, "Out of Time's Abyss: The Martian Stories of Edgar Rice Burroughs, A Speculation," *Riverside Quarterly* 4.2 (January 1970): 110-122.

20. Richard Lupoff, *Edgar Rice Burroughs: Master of Adventure* (New York: Acė Books, 1968), revised and enlarged edition. In French, Francis Lacassin has written a book-length study on Tarzan alone, *Tarzan, ou le Chevalier Crispé*, (Paris: Christian Bourgois, 1971). Lacassin's approach is partly biographical of Burroughs, partly interpretative of the novels, and partly devoted to Tarzan in the media.

Chapter 1

1. John Seeyle in his review of Irwin Porges' biography of Burroughs, *New York Times Book Review* 80 (26 October 1975): 38.

2. Here and elsewhere I owe a debt to Porges' book, *Edgar Rice Burroughs, The Man Who Created Tarzan* (Provo, Utah: Brigham Young University Press, 1975), for his work at almost every turn supports my views on the relationship between the heroic literature of antiquity and Burroughs' creation. Porges has made it possible on external grounds to document and trace the line of stylistic and narrative descent that I base on internal arguments arising out of Burroughs' text alone.

3. Porges, *Edgar Rice Burroughs,* pp. 17, 26, 27, 149, 194, 721 note 10.

4. Ibid., p. 734 note 86.

5. Ibid., p. 132.

6. Ibid., pp. 12, 145, 194.

7. Ibid., p. 327.

8. Ibid., p. 212. See also pp. 276f., 393.

9. The following reminder about one of the greatest potential horror stories in the history of Western literature may be pertinent here. Few would disagree that the *Aeneid* of Vergil, the grandest of the Latin poets, is one of the half dozen supreme works of our tradition. In its own right, as we have seen, it is a reshaper of a tradition and an influence on subsequent tradition. Yet, Vergil left absolute and explicit instructions to his literary executors, Varius Rufus and Plotius Tucca, that the entire manuscript of his great poem be totally destroyed on his death, for he felt the poem was a failure as it stood. One may be extremely thankful that Rufus and Tucca betrayed their trust. The story serves as a pointed reminder that even a great author is not necessarily the best judge of his own work.

10. Porges, *Edgar Rice Burroughs*, pp. 202, 363f., *passim.*

11. Ibid., p. 329.

12. The fact that Burroughs wrote rapidly does not mean he did not plan. He made elaborate notes and even drawings as preparations for his writing, but once he started, he did write very fast. Even so, he appears to have given much thought to sentence structure and plotted it out in his mind before committing it to paper. But, again, once he started to put it on paper, speed was typical. Porges makes the following observation in the biography (p. 192).

His approach did not include rough drafts, a practice followed by many authors who then revise or polish their material. Instead, he reflected upon each sentence, carefully working out the structure in his mind. He might sit silent for a long while, meditating, head down, in intense concentration, before turning to type the complete sentence. With this method he seldom found it necessary to make changes.

Chapter 2

1. *The Raw and the Cooked: Introduction to a Science of Mythology*, Vol. 1 (New York: Harper Torchbook TB/1487, 1970).
2. There can be little doubt that Burroughs developed his synkristic approach from ancient literature, especially from his reading of Plutarch, to whom by his own admission he kept coming back (Irwin Porges, *Edgar Rice Burroughs: The Man Who Created Tarzan* [Provo, Utah: Brigham Young University Press, 1975], p. 194).
3. The appended material, while not an exhaustive listing of the animal similes in Burroughs, indicates the range that is found: Antelope (1.66, 3.94), ape (2.171, 4.135), beast (1.160, 2.154, 3.69, 6.135), bull (2.88, 4.87), cat (3.76, 4.197, 4.198, 6.167), caterpillar (5.47), deer (1.165, 3.48, 3.153, 6.135, 6.137), dog (1.8, 1.230, 3.25, 3.135, 4.126, 5.11, 6.132), eagle (4.134), bull (5.33), hornets (2.142), hound (3.36, 4.98), hyena (4.101), jackal (1.48), lion (3.87), lioness (1.23, 4.125), monkey (1.29, 6.123), panther (1.149), pig (2.94), pigeon (5.156), rabbit (2.145, 3.104), sheep (2.127, 2.209, 3.53, 6.174), snake (1.35, 3.111, 3.132), squirrel (6.152), tigress (1.156, 4.158), and wolf (1.155).
4. See my paper, "Ring Composition and the *Persae* of Aeschylus," *Symbolae Osloenses* 45 (1970): 5–23.
5. Henry R. Immerwahr, *Form and Thought in Herodotus*, Philological Monographs 23 (Western Reserve Press, 1966), especially Ch. 2, "Style and Structure." See Galen O. Rowe, "Dramatic Structure in Caesar's *Bellum Civile*," *Transactions and Proceedings of the American Philological Association* 97 (1967): 399ff.

Chapter 3

1. Irwin Porges, *Edgar Rice Burroughs: The Man Who Created Tarzan* (Provo, Utah: Brigham Young University Press, 1975), pp. 75, 282, 364, 366, and *passim*.

2. See the discussion of this passage in E. R. Dodds, *The Greeks and the Irrational* (Berkeley, Calif.:University of California Press, 1951), Ch. 1.

3. W.K.C. Guthrie, *The Greeks and Their Gods* (Boston, Mass.: Beacon Press, 1956), pp. 113ff.

4. Porges, *Edgar Rice Burroughs*, pp. 75, 364.

5. Cited in ibid., p. 366. See all of p. 364 of Porges' biography; it contains much useful information. See also p. 282: ". . . Burroughs, as a man of science and a staunch believer in Darwin's theories. . . ."

6. Porges, *Edgar Rice Burroughs*, pp. 126, 142.

7. Ibid., p. 194.

8. Ibid.

9. Rudolph Altrocchi, *Sleuthing in the Stacks* (Cambridge: Harvard University Press, 1944), is far wide of the mark when he informs us that Kala's name is "more or less Congoesque" (p. 90).

Chapter 4

1. Fitzroy Richard Somerset, Lord Raglan, *The Hero: A Study in Tradition, Myth, and Drama* (New York: Vantage Books Inc., 1956), pp. 174f.

2. Irwin Porges, *Edgar Rice Burroughs: The Man Who Created Tarzan* (Provo, Utah: Brigham Young University Press, 1975), pp. 12, 129f.

3. Ibid., p. 399.

4. Ibid., p. 315f.

5. Ibid., p. 316.

6. The point is discussed at length by Brooks Otis in his *Vergil: A Study in Civilized Poetry* (Oxford: Oxford University Press, 1964), pp. 41ff. Otis calls the style subjective.

7. Bernard Fenik, *Typical Battle Scenes in the Iliad: Studies in the Narrative Technique of Homeric Battle Description*, HERMES Zeitschrift für Klassische Philologie, Einzelschriften, Heft 21 (Wiesbaden: F. Steiner, 1968). See especially pp. 6ff. for the immediate point.

8. Gore Vidal, "Tarzan Revisited," *Esquire* 60 (December 1963): p. 192ff., misses the point when he speaks only of Tarzan's control over the environment. Even more important is his self-control.

9. *The Trickster: A Study in American Indian Mythology* (New York: Bell Publishing Company, Inc., 1956).

10. Ibid., p. 132.
11. Ibid., p. ix.
12. Ibid., pp. ix, 124f., 133, 134f., 135, 139, 142, 185.
13. Ibid, p. 128.
14. For what we do know about his reading, see Porges, *Edgar Rice Burroughs*, pp. 132, 194, 213, 230.
15. Margaret Romer, "Edgar Rice Burroughs, Creator of Tarzan," *Overland Monthly* (March 1934): 67. Her article is apparently based on an interview she had with Burroughs on his Tarzana estate. Although she is not qualified to speak of the zoological or botanical accuracy of his jungle, she does make this observation: ". . . This jungle lore . . . is based on his careful study of many accounts of explorers and hunters in the African wilds."
16. John C. Cremony, *Life Among the Apaches* (San Francisco: A. Roman & Co., 1868); reprint, Tuscon: Arizona Silhouettes 1951; first trade edition, 1954.
17. Ibid., pp. 95f.
18. Ibid., p. 100.
19. Ibid., p. 101f.

Chapter 5

1. A summary of the genre can be found under the heading "Novel" in the *Oxford Classical Dictionary* (eds. N.G.L. Hammond and H. H. Scullard), second edition, 1970, pp. 739f. See also L. A. Post, *From Homer to Menander: Forces in Greek Poetic Fiction* (Berkeley, Calif.: University of California Press, 1951), especially pp. 156ff. The most useful modern survey in English of the genre is Ben Edwin Perry, *The Ancient Romances: A Literary-Historical Account of Their Origins* (Berkeley, Calif.: University of California Press, 1967). See also Arthur Heiserman, *The Novel Before the Novel: Essays and Discussions About the Beginnings of Prose Fiction in the West* (Chicago: University of Chicago Press, 1977).
2. The abduction is one of the "typical scenes" in Burroughs' novels, much as the battle scene, for example, is typical in the *Iliad* (see note 7 to Chapter 4). Each type has its formulas and its motifs, and the variations each author can play on the general type are virtually infinite. Repetitiveness in Burroughs is often held out as a major fault, while in Homer it has never prompted similar dissatisfaction. For a tabulation of these and similarly erotic scenes in Burroughs' earliest works, see Richard D. Mullen, "Edgar Rice Burroughs and the Fate Worse Than Death," *Riverside Quarterly* 4 (June 1970): 187ff.
3. A blow to Tarzan's head early in the novel (5.25) has caused amnesia, but throughout the book his "code" and behavior are consistent with the

norms established in the earlier novels. The book's later treatment of the relationship between Jane and various disreputable males who lust for her is reminiscent of Homer's treatment of Penelope and her suitors.

4. The literature on Darwin and Darwinism is truly enormous. For our purposes, the most useful single volume is Philip Appleman (ed.), *Darwin: A Norton Critical Edition* (New York: Norton, 1970). It contains essays and brief excerpts on Darwinism and on the impact of his theories on many other areas of thought, including literature.

5. Leo J. Henkin, *Darwinism in the English Novel 1869-1910: The Impact of Evolution on Victorian Fiction* (New York: Corporate Press, Inc. 1940). See especially Ch. 9, "The Anthropological Romance," pp. 168ff.

6. It is clear that the Greeks were familiar with the concept of evolution as early as Hesiod (eighth or seventh century B.C.), and Aristotle's ideas some three or four hundred years later were by no means original even in their nonspeculative origin. Useful is the discussion by Henry Fairfield Osborn, *From the Greeks to Darwin: An Outline of the Development of the Evolution Idea* (New York: Macmillan & Co., especially chs. 1 and 2).

7. *The Savage in Literature* (London: Routledge & K. Paul, 1975) p. 87.

8. George P. Elliott, "Getting Away from the Chickens," *Hudson Review* 12 (Fall 1959): 390.

9. See Brooks Otis, *Ovid as an Epic Poet* (Cambridge: Cambridge University Press, 1966), pp. 261ff. Also William S. Anderson, "Multiple Change in the Metamorphoses," *Transactions and Proceedings of the American Philological Association* 94 (1963): 1ff.

10. The classically educated Burroughs may have consciously made the woman's name end "-aya." It is an easy transliteration of the Greek *aia* (pronounced "aya"), a word that appears in Homer (for example, in *Odyssey* 11.301) and means "earth." In the Greek, myth the "earth" (g-aia) is the mother, and Burroughs may perhaps have enjoyed making up the Anglo-Greek appellative calque, Mom-aya, that is, Mother Earth. It would not be inconsistent with his sense of verbal humor. (See my comments on Kala's name in Ch. 3.)

11. Robert W. Fenton, *The Big Swingers* (Englewood Cliffs, N.J.: Prentice-Hall, 1967), p. 11.

BIBLIOGRAPHY

Altrocchi, Rudolph. *Sleuthing in the Stacks*. Cambridge: Harvard University Press, 1944.

Amis, Kingsley. *New Maps of Hell: A Survey of Science Fiction*. New York: Harcourt, Brace, 1960.

Anderson, William S. "Multiple Change in the Metamorphoses." *Transactions and Proceedings of the American Philological Association* 94 (1963): 1ff.

Appleman, Philip (ed.). *Darwin: A Norton Critical Edition*. New York: Norton, 1970.

Barmeyer, Eike. *Science-Fiction: Theorie und Geschichte*. Munich: W. Fink, 1972.

Birrell, Francis. "The Glories of Excess." *The New Statesman and Nation* (21 May 1932): 661f.

Boston Transcript, 14 September 1920. (Review of *Tarzan the Untamed*).

Boston Transcript, 21 March 1932. (Review of *Pirates of Venus*.)

Cremony, John C. *Life Among the Apaches*. San Francisco: A Roman & Co., 1868; reprint, Tucson: By Arizona Silhouettes, 1951.

Dodds, E. R. *The Greeks and the Irrational*. Berkeley, Calif.: University of California Press, 1951.

Elliott, George. "Getting Away from the Chickens." *Hudson Review* 12 (Fall 1959): 386–396.

Ewen, Edward T. "Eh-wa-au-wau-aoooow." *New York Times*, 23 September 1962, p. 57.

Fenik, Bernard. *Typical Battle Scenes in the Iliad: Studies in the Narrative*

Techniques of Homeric Battle Description. HERMES Zeitschrift für Klassische Philologie, Einzelschriften, Heft 21. Wiesbaden: F. Steiner, 1968.

Fenton, Robert W. *The Big Swingers.* Englewood Cliffs, N.J.: Prentice-Hall, 1967.

Flautz, John T. "An American Demagogue in Barsoom." *Journal of Popular Culture* 1 (1967): 263–275.

Green, Roger Lancelyn. *Into Other Worlds: Space-Flight in Fiction, From Lucian to Lewis.* London: Abelard-Schuman, 1958.

Guthrie, W.K.C. *The Greeks and Their Gods.* Boston: Beacon Press, 1956.

Hammond, N.G.L., and Scullard, H. H. *Oxford Classical Dictionary.* 2d edition, 1970. Oxford: Clarendon Press.

Heiserman, Arthur. *The Novel Before the Novel: Essays and Discussions About the Beginnings of Prose Fiction in the West.* Chicago: University of Chicago Press, 1977.

Henkin, Leo J. *Darwinism in the English Novel 1860–1910: The Impact of Evolution on Victorian Fiction.* New York: Corporate Press, Inc., 1940.

Holtsmark, Erling B. "Ring Composition and the *Persae* of Aeschylus." *Symbolae Osloenses* 45 (1970): 5–23.

Immerwahr, Henry R. *Form and Thought in Herodotus.* Philological Monographs 23. Cleveland: Western Reserve Press, 1966.

Independent (82), 19 April 1915. (Review of *Return of Tarzan.*)

Kyle, Richard. "Out of Time's Abyss: The Martian Stories of Edgar Rice Burroughs, A Speculation." *Riverside Quarterly* 4.2 (January 1970): 110–122.

Lacassin, Francis. *Tarzan, ou le Chevalier Crispé.* Paris, France: Christian Bourgois, 1971.

Lacon-Watson, E. H. "'Tarzan' and Literature." *Fortnightly* 119 (23 June 1923): 1035–1045.

Levinsen, Henrik. "'Vildmanden Tarzan' af Edgar R. Burroughs." *Børne-og ungdomsbøger: Problemer og analyser.* Copenhagen: Gyldendal, 1969, pp. 139–147 (edited by Sven M. Kristensen and Preben Ramlov).

Levi-Strauss, Claude. *The Raw and the Cooked: Introduction to a Science of Mythology.* New York: Harper and Row, 1970.

Lupoff, Richard. *Edgar Rice Burroughs: Master of Adventure.* New York: Ace Books, 1968.

McGreal, Dorothy. "The Burroughs No One Knows." *The World of Comic Art* 1.2 (Fall 1966): 12–15.

Mandel, Paul. "Tarzan and the Paperbacks." *Life* (29 November 1963), p. 11.

Mullen, Richard D. "Edgar Rice Burroughs and the Fate Worse Than Death" *Riverside Quarterly* 4 (June 1970): 187ff.

Nation (102), 6 April 1916. (Review of *Beasts of Tarzan.*)

Osborn, Henry Fairfield. *From the Greeks to Darwin: An Outline of the Development of the Evolution Idea* (New York: MacMillan & Co. 1913).

Otis, Brooks. *Ovid as an Epic Poet.* Cambridge: Cambridge University Press, 1966.

_____. *Vergil: A Study in Civilized Poetry.* Oxford: Clarendon Press, 1964.

Perry, Ben Edwin. *The Ancient Romances: A Literary-Historical Account of their Origins.* Berkeley, Calif.: University of California Press, 1967.

Porges, Irwin. *Edgar Rice Burroughs: The Man Who Created Tarzan.* Provo, Utah: Brigham Young University Press, 1975.

Post, L. A. *From Homer to Menander: Forces in Greek Poetic Fiction.* Berkeley, Calif.: University of California Press, 1951.

Rabkin, Eric S. *The Fantastic in Literature.* Princeton, N.J.: University of Princeton Press, 1976.

Radin, Paul. *The Trickster: A Study in American Indian Mythology.* New York: Philosophical Library, 1956.

Raglan, Lord. *The Hero: A Study in Tradition, Myth, and Drama.* New York: Vintage Books, Inc. 1956.

Romer, Margaret. "Edgar Rice Burroughs, Creator of Tarzan." *Overland Monthly* (March 1934): 67

Rowe, Galen O. "Dramatic Structure in Caesar's *Bellum Civile,*" *Transactions and Proceedings of the American Philological Association* 97 (1967): 399ff.

Seeyle, John. Review of Irwin Porges' *Edgar Rice Burroughs: The Man Who Created Tarzan, New York Times Book Review* 80 (26 October 1975): 26, 38.

Slate, Tom. "ERB and the Heroic Epic." *Riverside Quarterly* 3 (March 1968): 118–123.

Springfield Republican, 17 August 1924. (Review of *The Land That Time Forgot.*)

Street, Brian V. *The Savage in Literature: Representations of "Primitive" Society in English Fiction 1858–1920.* London: Routledge & K. Paul, 1975.

Vidal, Gore. "Tarzan Revisited." *Esquire* 60 (December 1963): 192–93, 262, 264.

INDEX OF NAMES,
PLACES AND SUBJECTS

INDEX OF PASSAGES CITED

From the Tarzan novels: the number(s) in front of the colon refer(s) to the page(s) of the novel, the number(s) after the colon refer(s) to the page(s) of this book on which the citation is found.

RETURN

17:102
25-26:108-9
28:117
29:102
32:102, 117
41:103
44:138
45:138
46:139
48:102
105:59
116:59
119:61
133:161

141:103
149:59
150:59
159:59
160:59
160-211:45-46
161:98
162:98
174:59-60
175:60
183:59, 60
184:137
190:68, 86
219:117, 140

BEASTS

7:95
13:28
16:148
26:14
43:49

69:134
80:102, 161
81:102
87:55
112:14

SON

13:79, 147
30:79
50:14
112-13:118
113:118

115:118
130:149
132:118
142:118
222:144

JEWELS

10:20
15:49

65:136
90:102

20:161
22:99
37:25
41:136
60:162
64:54

104:38-39
105:114
116:27
137:56
157:44

TALES

8:107
11:131
13:23
16:71
17:112
21:107
22:103
23:62
24:86
37:107
47:162
49:111
53:111
58:105
59-60:39-40
61:85, 104
63:112
64:112
70:14

106:107
108:116
124:122
126:123
128:123
134:110
138:110
141:111, 162
152:107
159:107
163:103
165:103
174:107
180-81:57-58
184:87
187:87
189:125
190-91:128
191:125

From ancient literature (includes passages discussed but not necessarily cited): same principle of citation as in the above.

HOMER ILIAD

1.493ff.:65-66
3.30ff.:105
4:460ff.:163
4.502ff.:163

13.397ff.:164
15.650ff.:163
16.258:106
16:332ff.:164

5.40ff.:163
5.590:106
8.258ff.:163-64
10.455ff.:164

17.132ff.:56
20.32:106
20.164ff.:105
20:475ff.:164

ODYSSEY

1.206ff.:81
1.296ff.:77
1.356ff.:78
5.206ff.:137
6.148:113
10.330ff.:137
11.1ff.:98

12.134ff.:124
17.304:116
19.273ff.:124
22.232:116
22.473:114
23.475ff.:114

VERGIL AENEID

1.159-68:12
6.126ff.:98

6.268:99
8.626-728:38

About the Author

ERLING B. HOLTSMARK is Associate Professor of Classics at the University of Iowa. His articles have appeared in *Hermes, Classical World, Journal of Popular Culture, Symbolae Osloenses,* and other scholarly publications.